A
GIRL'S GUIDE
TO
PERSONAL FINANCE

by

NANETTE JOELL (JOEY) BEECH

Published by Dvorkey, LLC, Ankeny, Iowa
ISBN: 978-0-9989207-0-2
Library of Congress Control Number: 2017906083

Edited by Sara Stibitz
Cover design and images by Juls Design
Author photograph by Ryan Damman
Layout by Guido Henkel

TO MY MOM
for teaching me the most
important lessons in life

TO MY HUSBAND AND KIDS
for being the source of joy in my life

TABLE OF CONTENTS

If we want to achieve our goal,
then let us empower ourselves
with the weapon of knowledge.

Malala Yousafzai

Preface

Money won't create success,
the freedom to make it will.

Nelson Mandela

Money doesn't buy happiness or health, but it does buy everything else. It buys food, clothing, shelter, transportation, insurance, education and entertainment. It is the driving force behind every business. It motivates our politics. And it is used to show social status. Whatever your opinion is regarding money and those who have it or don't have it, the fact is in America, money is important in day-to-day life.

Now that we have women across America making money, they need to know how to manage it. Certainly, having money is the goal, at least for me. But what gives me a sense of independence is the knowledge that if everything was gone tomorrow, I would know what to do to get back on my feet.

Freedom and independence have a different meaning to different people. To me freedom is the ability to make my own choices and go my own way. Far too many women have made sad, life-altering decisions based on financial need. My mother was one of them. When she was 28, she had two young children and was pregnant with me when she found out my father was cheating on her. She had one year of college and little work experience outside of our home. So, she stayed. She stayed with my father and tried to make the best of it. It wasn't until I was 11 years old that she finally kicked him out.

What made her stay with a man who cheated on her for almost 12 years and regularly humiliated her in public? Lack of money and the need to keep a roof over her kids' heads. Kicking my father out was the start of many long, hard years of financial struggles. At the time, she was an administrative assistant for the local school district. Once she kicked Dad out, she knew all the bills were her responsibility, and there was no way the hourly wage at the school was going to keep up a house and three kids.

Our financial future was bleak. Every time the car broke down or the furnace needed more oil, we were set further back. To breakeven would have been a huge blessing, but my father refused to pay child support or alimony. As a result, with every pair of gym shoes or household repair, the financial hole got deeper.

Through it all, Mom worked hard to keep us kids together. Thus, I was raised to be financially independent. Mom would always tell me, "Never get married until you can afford to raise three kids on your own."

That advice took on another form after Mom got a corporate job where reorganizations and layoffs were common. Mom did well there, and her hard work allowed her to not only get her financial footing, but also eventually build up her savings so she could purchase a home of her own. It was a good job but she was always aware of the reality that on any day the company could be sold, her department relocated, or her paycheck could be taken away by many other corporate means. She always said, "Save your money. Keep up your skills and network. Don't take for granted your paycheck will be there tomorrow."

Put another way, you never want to be one person or one situation away from welfare. Because it was so tough, Mom always dreamed of having a "Go to Hell" fund. To mom, a Go to Hell fund meant having enough money that she could tell a man or a company or anyone who mistreated her to "Go to hell." To Mom, money equaled freedom.

Financial security and freedom is very personal and different for everyone. Following the exact steps of someone else isn't going to get you to YOUR goal. Following such a plan will get you to someone else's version of financial security. This book provides the concepts and knowledge so you can make the best decisions for you each step of the way.

The concepts, tools and information in this book are here to help guide you, but **the journey is yours**. Where you go and how you get there will be determined by how you apply these tools and concepts in your life.

Section 1
Money Isn't Everything

Having money isn't everything, not having it is.

Kanye West

Money impacts and drives almost every aspect of your life, yet it is a taboo subject in most social settings, particularly among women.

Our everyday lives are filled with social perceptions, stereotypes, and myths associated with having or not having money. They are embedded in songs, comedy and the news we listen to daily. We often demonize the haves and the have-nots without knowing them at all. Being aware of your own perceptions about money will go a long way in your financial well-being.

Chapter 1
Why Money Matters

*Money doesn't buy happiness, but somehow it's
much more comfortable crying in a Porsche than
on a bicycle.*

Unknown

All the financial information in this book applies equally to either gender. After all, money itself is gender neutral. It doesn't matter if it is in a purse or a back pocket. Green is an appropriately gender neutral color.

I focus on women in this book because almost 35 years after my mother raised my siblings and me alone, society still doesn't do enough to equip girls and young women with the financial information needed in America today. And now that my daughter is starting out on her own I want her, and other young women like her, to have the information they need to live financially secure lives.

I give the same advice to my son. But my son has a few advantages over my daughter. He doesn't have the same social pressure to wear the latest fashion, spend a ton of money for make-up and hair styles, or even own more than one pair of shoes. As a boy, David was expected to do well in math and as a result, he did. My daughter, Gail, is smart and can learn anything she puts her mind to but there aren't many social points to be gained for girls in math class. Despite equal abilities, there seemed to be unequal expectations.

As average American parents, I'm sure my husband and I contributed to this expectation inequality. If Gail wanted to go to a movie my husband, Doug, handed her twenty dollars. If David wanted to go to a movie, Doug asked him if he had the money to go and where he thought he was going to get it.

Gail was also my shopping buddy. But it was like pulling teeth to get David to go shopping–even to get something he really needed, like dress pants for the dance he was going to in a few hours. We tried to treat them as equals when it came to money, but I'm sure they noticed subtle differences as they were growing up.

A Better World

I believe when we have more women who can manage their own finances with confidence, the better our world will be. They would enter relationships with a clear desire to be with their partner versus a financial need to be with their partner. Plus, they would have more to bring to the relationship. Financial literacy has been shown to improve mental health, long-term career success and personal relationships.

Financial literacy is low among both genders. It isn't being taught enough in our schools or our homes. With the constant deluge of information and rapid technology development in the last few decades, the everyday life lessons of money management got lost in the shuffle. As financial transactions shifted from face-to-face exchanges, to faceless online transactions, we lost the basic lessons of personal finance.

If we elevate the knowledge of one gender, we can positively impact the knowledge of both genders. Then both genders can lead by example and carry the lessons on to future generations.

I am not here to debate or discuss the reasons behind gender inequality, but it clearly exists. I simply intend to provide a resource to young women to help level the financial playing field.

Young women are at a financial disadvantage. Most reports have women earning between 77 and 91 percent of what men are earning.[1] On top of that disparity in pay, there is the pink tax.[2] The pink tax is the label for the pricing practice where products marketed to females cost more than the same product marketed to males. The most common example is razors. A package of pink razors marketed toward women is more expensive and contains fewer than the package of blue razors marketed toward men. The razors are the same except for the color. Multiple reports in the U.S. and Europe have confirmed these pricing discrepancies, with price differences between 4 to 50% higher for the product marketed toward women.

The problem is not just the price of female-oriented products but the massive marketing that bombards women daily to get us to buy these products. From hygiene to houses, the marketing push on us is relentless.

Recently, a popular women's magazine was left in the seat pocket of an airplane I was on during a trip. On the cover, it had Jennifer Aniston, who played Rachel Green in my all-time favorite TV show, *Friends*. So, I picked it up and looked for the story about the woman whose hair I tried to duplicate in my 20's. I flipped through the pages, eager to read about the woman I had watched for years.

I struggled to find the story about her. In fact, I struggled to find any story or content page at all! This wasn't my first magazine. I have managed to navigate many magazines in my life. But finding the cover article in this magazine was like an extreme version of Where's Waldo.

During my search I got so disgusted with the lack of any content other than ads I gave up looking for the article altogether. I decided instead to count the number of pages that were predominately advertising. I soon came to the conclusion it would be easier to count the number of pages that had more content than advertising.

Of the 274 pages, a mere 62 were non-ad pages. That means the $6 magazine is 77% ads! That's like watching 45 minutes of commercials to see 15 minutes of a show. Unless it is the Super Bowl, where the commercials can be as entertaining as the game itself, no one would waste their time with it.

I did finally find the table of contents. It was on page 66 and was basically a large purse ad with a list of articles wedged in the margins.

When I shared this story with my 20-year-old son, he pulled out a recent issue of a popular sports magazine he regularly reads. The target audience for his magazine is men. He found most of the content is upfront and easy to find. About 70% of his magazine is content and only 30% advertising. In addition, most of the advertising was toward the back of the magazine.

This is just a small-scale example. The tactics marketers use to separate you from your money are endless and ever-changing. Online, the tricks are even more elaborate. As a result, it is often hard to know what and who to believe. As if earning money wasn't hard enough, in America today keeping your money can be just as difficult.

The principles in this book apply to all ages, but the examples are focused on young women. I want to provide the resources I wished were available to my daughter, Gail, when she asked for help as she was leaving college and starting her first full-time job.

She's one of the lucky ones. She got a degree without a lot of debt. She is a well-informed and rounded person. She keeps up on the news, reads a variety of blogs and makes use of online resources. But when she was signing up for employee benefits and looking for a place of her own, she had a lot of questions. Where to live? How much rent could she afford? Can she afford her own place or would she need a roommate?

Should she sign up for the retirement plan? What about the medical coverage? Can she afford to save for graduate school?

Gail is not alone. Her cousins, friends and classmates are all facing similar challenges. There is a great crop of young women currently entering the workforce. They have enormous talent and skills. But sadly, the predominant messages our society has for them are about fashion, home décor and pop culture. Our society offers more to young women about how to decorate their apartment than how to pay for their apartment.

A lot of the available information about money is provided by financial firms, which stand to profit from the decisions these young women are making. These can be great resources, but they fall short of being objective. Our young people deserve sound financial information to help them make the best financial decisions possible. Their future is bright. I want to help them shine as brightly as possible.

According to a recent study, women will control close to 75% of discretionary spending worldwide by 2028.[3] That is a lot of economic power! Let's use it wisely. The influence our spending habits have can literally shift economies.

Discretionary spending is the spending beyond the necessities. Movie tickets, home decor, cocktails, luxury soaps, lotions and candles and things not required to support daily living are considered discretionary. I would argue women also have significant influence on nondiscretionary spending, like housing, utilities, food and other necessities.

How are we going to use this influence? Are we going to make sure our families and communities are financially stable? Or are we going to drown in debt and hope someone bails us out? It sounds melodramatic but I believe the economic power women hold can be the positive influence our families and communities need.

Keeping It Simple!

In this book, I intentionally keep it simple. If you can understand and apply core financial concepts, you have what you need to live a financially successful life.

Being financially stable has far more to do with basic knowledge and good spending habits than with your income or math abilities.

What matters most is that you understand the big picture of your finances. If you round up your expenses and round down your income, managing to the very penny isn't going to matter. You'll have money in the bank.

Some get a runner's high when working out. Others get a high from creating the perfect spreadsheet. If you want to have extensive spreadsheets and read every word of your account statements, great. Have at it. But it isn't required.

Financial well-being is about the big concepts and how you apply them day-to-day.

It's not about the math or knowing how to create complex spreadsheets. **It's about understanding your income and knowing what to do with it.** Yes, this book covers the math and includes spreadsheets. These are offered to make a point and show you how to do the math yourself. But they are just tools to help you accomplish your goal, like a calendar to manage your time or a contact system to manage phone numbers. **The best spreadsheet in the world isn't going to help if you can't control your spending.**

I know people who have never balanced their checkbook but still have a net worth of well over $2 million dollars. And they started out in entry-level jobs and in debt. They didn't become millionaires by balancing their checkbook to the penny every month. They got there by following the golden rules of finance. They watched what they spent and made saving a priority.

This book isn't about taking some extreme position on finance. I'm not going to tell you all debt is bad, never splurge on a vacation, or stay home every night counting your pennies. Healthy management of your money is a balance, like maintaining a healthy weight. It allows you to indulge on a hot fudge sundae now and then. If you have a fudge sundae every night, it wouldn't be as satisfying and you'd likely be in poor health with extra pounds. Managing your money is the same way. You need to watch what you spend most days so you can occasionally splurge and enjoy it.

With this book, I explain how finance works so you know how to make the right decisions throughout your life.

If you finish this book and want to learn more, there is a list of resources in the Tools and Resources chapter at the end. I encourage you to use them and other reliable sources to educate yourself. These and other resources are also available at AGirlsGuideToPersonalFinance.com.

Remember, it is not about how much you make, it is about what you do with what you make.

Chapter 2
What Money Is and What It Isn't

When you know better you do better.

Maya Angelou

Net Worth ≠ Personal Worth

Net worth and personal worth are not the same. It is important to know the difference.

Your *net worth* is a number. It is the mathematical number that represents the value of all you own minus all you owe. Your *net worth* is a mathematical measurement of what you own. It is the result of the equation Assets – Liabilities = Net Worth.

Your *personal worth* is the value of what you are, your character and the talents you have to share. Your personal worth is your value to the world. It is who you are as a person, friend, family member, citizen and co-worker.

Never confuse your **personal worth** with your **net worth**.

In mid-2015 I was driving in downtown Des Moines. Compared to most U.S. cities, there aren't many homeless people or panhandlers in Des Moines, Iowa. But on this day, two were on the side of the road just off the interstate. One was a young woman. Mid-20's I'd guess. She held a sign that read, "Too proud to prostitute." While this is an extreme example, this young woman knew her lack of money didn't mean she had no worth as a person.

Most people are uncomfortable with this example. I get it. It's raw. And I don't agree with the approach or actions of the young lady, but it does help make the point.

Most of us have all swallowed our pride at some point in order to pay the bills. My mom swallowed her pride each day she stayed with my father. As a young cocktail waitress, I put up with male customers making rude and sexist comments while I did my job. In the corporate world, I witnessed women working insane hours, regularly sacrificing time with their husbands and kids to keep up with unrealistic workloads.

I believe money is very important, so important that it is worth writing a book about. But it is only one important aspect of our lives. Health, wellness, and relationships are also very important.

Financial savvy is sexy!

Don't believe the myths. You don't have to be a math wiz or nerd to have command of your finances. Financial savvy is sexy! Confidence looks good on everyone, and one of the surest ways to gain confidence is to have your financial house in order. There is a swagger that comes from living within your means and being financially stable.

If you have the money or at least the financial know-how to pay your own way, you are less likely to put up with a boyfriend or relative who is abusive, or a boss who doesn't treat you with respect. Money allows you the cushion and confidence to find a new place to live, time to find a new job, or the freedom to have dinner with someone whose company you enjoy.

Managing your money isn't only about looking out for number one; it is about taking personal responsibility. It's about taking care of yourself and your family. It's about old-fashioned wisdom to work hard, save, and help your neighbor when you can.

Since most careers involve a business or budget of some form, the more comfortable you are with the topics, the more value you can provide your employer. Those who understand finance and budgets are more likely to get promoted over those who aren't comfortable with conversations around money.

Income is Only Part of the Equation

Thomas J Stanley, PhD has done extensive research into the habits and happiness of those with high incomes. His research found those who spend above their means (income) tend to be dissatisfied with their lives. Those who live below their means are significantly more likely to report that they are happy.[1] Research also shows those spending above their income to keep up with their friends and neighbors are unhappy, despite having a strong income. Findings show they would be significantly happier living in a moderate-income neighborhood than living in a higher-income neighborhood.

As Stanley's research points out, a person's happiness is less about the amount of money they make and more about the people with whom they surround themselves or compare themselves. His research shows instead of being happy in a dream home in the expensive neighborhood, you may end up being just the opposite. Money not only doesn't buy happiness, but sometimes it actually buys misery.

Chapter 3
The Math is Simple!

Life is really simple,
but we insist on making it complicated.

Confucius

It Is the Self-discipline that Is Hard

Far too many girls still shy away from math in far larger numbers than boys. However, there is no evidence that males are better at math than females. And, too often girls assume if they didn't master advanced math subjects like algebra and calculus they can't master finance. **Personal finance is just simple math applied to money matters.**

Good news: no advanced math is needed! No algebra, no calculus, no trigonometry, no geometry! Eighty percent of personal finance is nothing more than adding and subtracting. The other twenty percent is simple multiplication and division. Any Dollar Store calculator can handle the calculations for you. Even better, every smart phone has a calculator that can do the calculations for you. There are apps for it as well.

Trust me. No matter what grades you got in math class, *you can do it.* You can effectively manage your money and take control of your financial life. If you can master the following equation, you have the foundation to be rich. If you don't master it, debt will always be a part of your life, and will likely control it.

Income – Expenses = Gain (or Loss)

Like sports or video games, if you have too many losses you'll be out of the game. On the other hand, if you regularly have gains you will rack up wins and the odds start tipping in your favor. The more wins you rack up, the easier it becomes. If you master your money you will find you have choices you never imagined!

The formula doesn't change when you put dollar signs in front of the numbers. Yet, for some reason, how we approach the formula does change. There is something that clouds our minds, or more likely, our emotions, when the formula includes the almighty dollar sign. The more you can separate the emotion from the math, the easier it gets to manage your money.

Income minus expenses is the magic formula. It is the scoreboard of your financial life. This is one of the few things in life you can have a direct impact on. If you work more and increase your income, you improve your bottom line. Reduce your expenses and you get the same effect. You have influence over the outcome. Use it!

The term "bottom line" comes from the fact that it is the last line of the equation, the bottom line of an income statement or a net worth calculation. The bottom line is showing you how much you are gaining or losing. It has become a common term used to refer to the end result or the outcome, so it is a great term to refer to your financial results.

If you listen to financial talk shows you may hear the term "top line." This is used to refer to the income portion of the equation. Your top line is the money you have coming in. Your bottom line is what you have left after expenses (what you spend).

I want to be clear. Managing your money doesn't mean balancing your checking account. You can balance your account to the penny, but that's just doing a math problem. Managing your money is about influencing and directing your income and expenses. While keeping track of both is important, **it is more about the choices you make and less about the bookkeeping.** If you make good choices about your expenses in relation to your income, the bookkeeping gets really easy. And like any game, it can even be fun as you improve your score. The more you practice, the easier it gets.

Understanding the numbers is key, but that doesn't mean you have to be an accountant or math enthusiast. With today's technology, almost instant account access, and prompt execution of transactions, all you have to do is log into your account to know where you stand—assuming you remember the spending that hasn't cleared the bank yet.

Of course, you have to keep track of income and expenses, but it isn't about having organized file folders and sharp pencils. It's about knowing your numbers and sticking to your financial priorities. A simple budget will make your numbers obvious and help you keep on track. It will also give you confidence in situations that can otherwise be intimidating.

Math doesn't lie. It just keeps score. If your expenses are more than your income, you are in negative territory. If you are in negative territory month after month, year after year, your debt will pile up. It all adds up and it will take an equal or greater amount of income to get rid of debt.

In Chapter 8: Budget to Know Where You Are, we'll talk about everything you need to draft your budget. For now, just know budgeting and spending wisely doesn't mean you are cheap. It means you value money and don't want to waste it.

Loans and the associated interest is where most of the multiplication and division comes into play, and we'll cover those in the section called Keeping What You Earn, where you will see how paying interest works against you. Then, in the Make Your Money Grow section, you will see how the same math can work for you instead of against you.

Section 2
Keeping What You Earn

Freedom's just another word for nothin' left to lose.

Janis Joplin, *Me and Bobby McGee*

In Thomas J Stanley's book, *Millionaire Women Next Door,* and his other related works, he clearly dispels the myth that having a high income equals having a high net worth. His research shows that those with high incomes often have surprisingly low net worth. Their spending habits are so high that they exceed their unusually high incomes. They are often less happy than lower income earning peers. The research shows some of the richest people live in humble homes and frequently shop at discount stores like Wal-Mart.[1] That's part of how they got rich!

The next ten chapters are focused on how to keep what you earn so you can enjoy it. The information and suggestions are offered so you can be financially successful at any income level. This section includes practical knowledge and is coupled with ways to establish and maintain good financial habits that will benefit you throughout life.

Chapter 4
Pay Yourself First

A penny saved is a penny earned.

Benjamin Franklin

How Much You Keep is More Important than How Much You Make

Women tend to take care of those around them first, often putting the needs of others before their own. This is a good quality, but if we don't take care of our own financial well-being, we will someday be dependent on the financial well-being of someone else and their willingness to take care of us.

Paying yourself first is advice that has been handed down for centuries. It means you should regularly set some money aside for yourself. I imagine it came from the universal fact there are always plenty of friends, relatives or make-up counter sales staff who would like some of your money. If you don't put some aside for yourself, you'll quickly find everyone has your money but you.

To some, paying yourself first sounds selfish. It isn't. It's like the flight attendant's reminder to put your oxygen mask on first before you help those around you. You can't help others if you haven't first taken care of yourself.

Like brushing your teeth in the morning, it has to be an ingrained habit, so ingrained that not doing it would feel awkward and wrong. If it isn't ingrained, something will always come up and get in the way of saving.

To establish and maintain a habit of saving, make it as easy on yourself as possible. Direct deposit and automatic transfers can save you time, hassle and money. If your employer allows you to direct deposit your paycheck into more than one account, do it! A simple but efficient way to handle this is to put the amount you need to cover your living expenses in a checking account and the remaining in a savings account. It is easy to move some savings to checking if needed. It is much harder to move what is left over into savings. It rarely happens because there is always something we'd like to have that feels more fun in the moment.

Here is an example of how this works. Ashley is a young woman who recently graduated from college and got a job in her chosen field. Ashley has monthly living expenses of $1,940. She is paid twice a month. She has half of her monthly expenses ($970) from each paycheck deposited into her checking account and the remainder of her paycheck ($154.56) goes into her savings account. This way, Ashley manages her spending based on her expected and planned expenses, NOT on how much is in her paycheck. If an unexpected expense or opportunity comes up she can pull money from her savings, if needed.

Ashley wants to replace her car in the next few years. As she is saving up for a new car, any unplanned expense is mentally weighed against the desire for a new car. The hot concert ticket may or may not be worth postponing the purchase of a car.

This automatic savings plan makes it harder to go over budget because it requires more effort to interrupt than if all her money was in the same checking account. That little additional effort to transfer funds may be just enough to keep Ashley from making an impulsive purchase. Plus, any expense taken from her savings account is mentally evaluated against her desire for a new car.

Another BIG advantage of fixing her deposit locations and amounts comes into play when Ashley gets a raise. When Ashley's income goes up, her expenses remain the same. This means that her savings will automatically go up. More per paycheck will go into her savings account, making the new car easier to reach. When she gets a bonus at the end of the year, the same will happen. The living expenses ($970) will continue to go into her checking and the (now increased) remainder into her savings. This gives her additional money in her savings account to eventually treat herself for her hard work. Any amount over $970 will go into her savings, with no additional effort on her part.

The more automatic your savings, the faster it will add up. This in turn reinforces the habit. There are always expenses and they are easy to justify. If you wait until all the expenses are paid and then save, you are almost guaranteed to have less left over for savings. You need a strong savings habit and instinct to protect you from all the ads and people who try to talk you into reducing your saving so you can buy a _____. Fill in the blank with any first world "need" that comes to mind (i.e., a flat screen, new cell phone, sonic blender, smaller laptop, upscale car, weekend away, pedicure).

Let's say Ashley also wants to take a trip next year with friends. She expects the trip will cost about $900. To make sure she has the money, she sets up another savings account. She then sets up an automatic monthly transfer of $75 from her regular savings account to her trip savings account.

With these automatic transfers, Ashley can focus on living her life. She knows that when it comes time to replace her car and take her trip, she'll have money to do both. She also isn't spending time each month wondering where all her money went. She'll automatically know. With automatic payments set up, she can spend 15 minutes a month reviewing it all and the rest of the month focused on other things.

A strong savings habit makes it easier to stave off temptation when those dream boots are on sale. Once a savings habit is established, failing to save starts to feel uncomfortable. Even if you can only save a couple of dollars to start, it is worth doing to build the habit of saving. Assuming you keep your expenses the same, as your income grows you will automatically increase your savings along with your increased income.

Chapter 5
Understanding Your Paycheck

Who is FICA? Why is he getting all of my money?

Rachel Green in *Friends*

With the excitement of a new job generally comes a blur of paperwork and benefit selection, not to mention what to wear, where to park, and where to find your desk.

Before you go shopping in anticipation of a big paycheck, remember that part of it will automatically be taken in taxes. Everyone earning an income has some taxes withheld. The Federal Insurances Contributions Act (FICA) sets a tax for employees and employers to fund Social Security (a base retirement income for "old" retired people) and Medicare (medical insurance for "old" people). On top of that there are federal income taxes and state income taxes, in most states. These taxes fund our federal, state and local governments and pay for things like schools, military/defense, roads, safety services and much more.

I'm not going to bore you with details about taxes. But it is important you are aware of them and take them into account. If you don't, you could find yourself in debt to Uncle Sam. Generally, you can expect taxes to take 10-30% of your paycheck depending on your income, exemptions, and other factors. Taxes, like other debts, penalties, interest, and fees can quickly get out of hand and pile-up if not resolved in a timely manner.

What matters is what you keep

Remember, Ashley, from the previous chapter? She just got a full-time job as a private middle school music teacher. Her new position provides a full insurance package (health, dental, vision), a 401(k)-retirement plan with an employer match, and a salary of $45,000. Following is one of her pay stubs. We will first look at it line by line at a high level. Later, we will dig into some of the topics in more detail.

1. Pay Period: The dates here are the days included in the pay period for this check (pay stub).

2. Tax Allowances: This line is a heading for the following three tax related lines, with a column for federal and state tax allowances.

3. Marital Status: The U.S. tax structure is based on households and as such applies different limits to married taxpayers and single taxpayers.

4. Allowances: There are tax breaks for those who take financial responsibility for themselves and others (i.e., spouse, children, financially dependent parents). The more allowances claimed, the less taxes will be withheld from your paycheck. If more taxes are withheld from your paycheck than are due, you'll receive a refund when you file your annual tax return. If not enough taxes are withheld (based on allowances claimed on W-4 form), you will owe money when you file your annual tax return.
Ashley claims 1 allowance when completing the W-4 form. The W-4 is a government-required form that is part of the paperwork when starting a new job. Had Ashley opted to claim zero allowances, it would result in the maximum withholding for her income.

Ashley's Pay Stub

1	Pay Period	Bi-weekly				
2	Tax Allowances	Federal	State			
3	Marital Status	Single	Single			
4	Allowances	1	1			
5	Additional Amount	$0.00	$0.00			

Direct Deposit(s)

		Bank Routing #	Account #		Amount	
6	Account Type	Bank Routing #	Account #		Amount	
7	Checking	123456789	9999999		$	970.00
8	Savings	123456789	8888888		$	154.56

Hours and Earnings

9	Regular Pay	$	1,730.77	Annual Salary of $45,000

Before-Tax Deductions

10	Medical coverage	$	45.00	
11	Dental Coverage	$	5.00	
12	Vision	$	2.50	
13	401(k)	$	103.85	6%
14	Flex Spending Medical	$	52.50	
	Total after deducts	$	**1,521.92**	

Taxes

15	Fed Withholding	$	181.98	
16	Fed Med/Ee	$	24.33	
17	Fed Social Sec/Ee	$	104.05	
18	State Withholding	$	77.00	
	Total Taxes	$	**387.36**	

After-Tax Deductions

19	United Way	$	10.00	
	Total After-Tax Deduct	$	**10.00**	

20	**Net Pay**	$	**1,124.56**	

Employer-Paid Benefits

21	Medical coverage	$	106.25	
22	Group Life Insurance	$	9.75	
23	Long-term Disability	$	13.00	
24	401(k)	$	51.93	50% match up to 6% **FREE money**

5. Additional Amount: If Ashley was concerned she will owe more taxes than what is being withheld, she can have an additional dollar amount withheld for taxes. As a result, she would owe less at the end of the year (or if she paid too much she will receive a bigger refund). Ashley already expects to get a refund so she doesn't want any more to be withheld.

6. Account Type: This is a heading line for the list of direct deposit accounts that follow it.

7. Checking: Ashley has monthly expenses of $1,940, so she has half this amount ($970) directly deposited into her checking account each bi-monthly paycheck. Any pay over the $970 goes into her savings account.

8. Savings: Any amount left over after the $970 Ashley has deposited into her checking account is automatically deposited into her savings ($154.56).

9. Regular Pay: This is the total amount Ashley was paid before any taxes or deductions were taken out.

10. Medical Coverage: This is the amount Ashley pays for her portion of her medical insurance through her employer. Medical coverage, as well as all of the other contributions in this section (medical, dental, vision, 401(k) and flex-spending accounts (line items 10-14)), are deducted from Ashley's pay prior to any taxes being applied. As a result, they cost her less than if they were paid for with after-tax dollars.

11. Dental Coverage: The amount Ashley pays for her portion of her dental insurance, which works much like medical coverage.

12. Vision: The amount Ashley pays for her vision insurance.

13. 401(k): The amount Ashley is contributing to her traditional 401(k)-retirement savings account.

14. Flex Spending Medical: The amount Ashley is putting into a Flex-Spending account for medical expenses she expects to pay throughout the calendar year. This is a savings account specifically designed to pay for medical expenses she expects to have during the calendar year. Any amount left over her actual allowable medical expenses will be lost, so she is careful not to over fund this account.

15. Fed Withholding: The amount withheld for federal income taxes.

16. Fed Med/Ee: The amount withheld for her portion of federal Medicare/Medicaid withholdings.

17. Fed Social Sec/Ee: The amount withheld for her portion of Social Security withholdings.

18. State Withholdings: The amount withheld for state income taxes in Ashley's state.

19. United Way: Through her employer Ashley donates $10 per pay period to the charity United Way.

20. Net Pay: The total amount of money Ashley receives after all the tax, benefit and charitable deductions. This is the amount Ashley actually receives and divides up between her savings and checking accounts.

21. The amounts listed under Employer-Paid Benefits (21-24) don't affect Ashley's pay. They simply show how much her employer is paying for its portion of her insurance coverage and 401(k) retirement account. Line 21 Medical Coverage is for her health insurance.

22. Group Life Insurance: Employer's portion of her life insurance coverage.

23. Long-term Disability: Employer's portion of her long-term disability insurance.

24. 401(k): The amount her employer contributed to Ashley's retirement account. More on this later in the chapter and in Chapter 15.

Direct Your Deposits

When you first start a job, there are many forms and processes to go through. At the same time that you select your benefits and complete your W-4 form, you are usually asked to set up electronic deposit of your pay. This is a simple but important step. It is an easy way to start your budgeting and increase the odds you'll be able to stick to it. It's where you designate how much of your pay goes into your checking and savings accounts. This is a great way to establish your savings habit.

If your employer allows you to designate more than one direct deposit account, I recommend doing what Ashley did in this example. Have the amount you need to cover set expenses deposited into your checking account. Have all the remaining money deposited into a savings account. You can change these account settings later if you need to, so don't put it off.

If your employer doesn't allow for multiple direct deposit accounts, you can accomplish the same thing by setting up an automatic transfer between your accounts at your bank. Go to your bank online or in-person and set up automatic transfer of the amount of your expected expenses from your savings account into your checking account the day after each payday. This accomplishes the same result as direct depositing into two separate accounts.

While at your bank (or on their web site) I highly recommend setting up overdraft protection. I have this set up with my personal accounts. If I ever make a mistake or an unexpected expense comes up that my checking account can't cover, which would cause an overdraft, my bank automatically transfers the amount of the short fall from my savings account into my checking account. Another common form of overdraft protection provides a short-term loan to cover a small shortfall.

Another way to avoid problems like overdrafts or running short is to have an extra $100 in your checking account (spending account). This provides a little buffer in case you forget something or an incidental expense comes up.

Overdrafts can happen if a check or other payment from your account is more than the amount in your account at the time it is processed. If you have an unexpected car repair on Tuesday and your rent is automatically paid out of your account on Wednesday, you could be in a tight (and embarrassing) spot with your landlord and your bank if your account doesn't have enough money or you don't have overdraft protection.

Overdraft protection won't provide funds where there aren't any. It simply transfers money between your accounts in case something comes up or you miscalculate an expense. There is a fee when this happens, but it is reasonable and less than overdraft fees. It also avoids the hassle of returned checks, the fees associated with them, and the possible hit to your credit score.

As fathers everywhere love to say, "Just because you have checks or a plastic card doesn't mean you have money." They may be old and crotchety but they have a way of making a point.

Employer Sponsored Insurance Plans

Group insurance plans available through an employer are generally less expensive than what you'd be able to purchase on your own for the same or similar coverage. Unless you have specific medical requirements or can find the same insurance at a lower rate somewhere else, you should purchase it through your employer.

At a minimum, **you should have medical coverage** and long-term disability insurance. A medical condition or long-term disability pose the most significant threat to your financial stability. They can impact both your ability to earn an income and are often associated with high expenses. These are the most important coverages to have because one accident can financially wipe you out.

Dental, vision, life, short-term disability and other insurance offerings from your employer should be evaluated based on your personal need for the coverage and the cost. If the cost is competitive, take advantage of it. In Chapter 13: Insure for a Good Night's Sleep, I talk more about common insurance coverage you will want to have.

Employer Sponsored Retirement Savings

The 401(k) plan is the most common employer-sponsored retirement account option, so we will focus on it. There are other retirement plans; if your employer offers one, take advantage of it. It will likely have some of the same advantages as a 401(k).

Included below are reasons why a qualified retirement account like a 401(k) plan is a great way to save. Note: when referring to retirement accounts, the term "qualified" refers to the account's status under the Federal law known as ERISA (Employee Retirement Income Security Act of 1974). A qualified account simply means the account qualifies under ERISA for tax-advantaged treatment that isn't allowed in accounts that don't qualify.

This tax-advantage status makes these plans a BIG deal. It is a deal you can't get anywhere else. If your employer doesn't offer a retirement plan you can setup an individual retirement account (IRA). Information about IRAs is included in Chapter 15.

Why 401(k) qualified retirement accounts are a great way to save.

1. Supports paying yourself first
2. Is simple and automatic
3. Many employers match your contributions, aka Free Money
4. Gets special tax treatment
5. Opportunity for investment gains
6. Puts your money out of sight and out of mind
7. There in case of emergency

Let's look at each of these reasons a little closer.

1. It supports the principal of **paying yourself first**. All the money you put in is yours. There are rules and limitations, but the money you put in is yours.

2. It is **simple and automatic**. Once you fill out the initial forms and select your investment options, contributions are automatically made with each paycheck. Little effort is needed on your part. The automatic deduction from your paycheck makes it easier to avoid the temptation of spending it on concert tickets or another pair of shoes.

3. **Many employers will match** a portion of the money you put into a 401(k). A common plan is to match 50% of every dollar you contribute up to six percent of your salary. So, if you contribute $100 per paycheck, your employer will contribute $50. This is a 50% return. Take advantage of it! It is free money.

   Yes, there are usually vesting requirements that say you don't get to keep the employer contributes until you stay employed with the company for a set number of years. But these schedules are generally reasonable given it is free money. No matter what, your contributions are yours the minute you make them.

4. Qualified retirement accounts receive **special tax treatment**. In the United States, having a community full of citizens who can pay their own way in retirement is so valued that the tax rules were designed to encourage everyone to save their money for it.

   With regard to 401(k) plans and IRAs, this special treatment comes in two forms known as the traditional (before tax) and Roth (after tax) options. If you select the traditional option, you don't pay taxes on the money you put in but you pay taxes when you withdraw money out of it. If you select the Roth option, you pay taxes on the money you put into the account on the front end, but you don't pay taxes on the money you withdraw from it (except dollars your employer contributes). Both options offer significant tax savings, so following a few rules is well worth it for the significant tax savings provided.

5. The **opportunity for investment gain** isn't unique to retirement accounts. Whenever you set aside money and invest it there is potential for gain and the potential for loss. What is unique to a qualified account is those gains aren't taxed in the year of the gain. This allows gains to compound as long as it is in the account.

   The structure and nature of an employer retirement plan makes it easy for you to gradually and regularly invest. This regular and gradual approach helps you get familiar with investing and can reduce your risk by spreading your investments out. A gradual and incremental approach is how many financial advisors and experts recommend you invest.

6. Money put into a retirement account is out of your everyday sight. **Out of sight, out of mind** is a common saying that means if you put something away out of your everyday view, you are less likely to think about it and use it. It is like the dress stuck in the back of your closet that you meant to wear; because you couldn't see it while you got dressed, you never wore it. Have you ever tried to hide cookies out of your sight so you wouldn't eat them all at once? The same concept applies to your money. If you put it away, you are less likely to consume it all after a bad day at work.

7. If an emergency does come up, you can take your money out. I highly discourage taking money out of a retirement account prior to retirement, but in the face of a true emergency, it is an option. Taxes and penalties will likely apply.

   In a way, it could act as a back-up emergency account in case the worst does happen. Had you not saved the money, you would have paid the taxes straight out of your paycheck anyway. The 10% penalty on early withdrawals is like a protective fence around your savings; it makes you think twice before you grab it. It makes you consider other options first, which often results in creative solutions.

Another option in case of an emergency is a loan from your account. Most plans allow participants to borrow as much as half of their account balance, up to $50,000. A reasonable interest rate would apply and you must pay it back within five years. It may also come due immediately if you leave the employer for any reason, including job loss. For this reason, loans aren't recommended and should only be used when facing an emergency with no other available solution.

It is important to understand what is taken out of your paycheck so you can control where your money goes. It is also wise to take advantage of the benefits your employer offers. For most, your paycheck is the foundation of your financial life. It reflects your income, benefits, taxes and often how much you put toward savings and expenses.

Now that you've seen Ashley's paycheck, take a few minutes to look at your own. Go through it line-by-line. If there is something you don't understand or aren't sure of, ask. You'll get the most out of your paycheck when you understand it and direct it toward your priorities.

Chapter 6
Credit – Know the Score

*It takes many good deeds to build
a good reputation, and only one bad one to lose it.*

Benjamin Franklin

Give Yourself Some Credit

"Would you like to put this on your store credit card?" seems like a perfectly innocent question when the clerk at the checkout asks it. Why is it some store clerks always ask this question? Did they all get together in the break room and say, "Hey, let's all ask our customers this same question?" Why do these same retailers (airlines, online stores and the like) offer significant discounts and "rewards" to those who sign-up for and use their credit card offers? Is it they like you to have something in your wallet with their brand name on it? Maybe. Could it also be that in the process they gain information about your purchasing habits that helps them market more of their services to you? Maybe it's because people often buy more when they are charging on a credit card than when they are taking money directly out of their wallet or account (via debt card)? My guess is all but the break room conversation apply.

Why they ask this question isn't as important as what you hear in your head when they do. Do you hear, "Yippee, more rewards and savings for me?" Or, "Yes, I want to delay paying for these items as long as I can." Or do you hear, "No thanks. I prefer to keep my money and information to myself."

I generally find the nicest response to this question and others like it is, "No, thank you." It is not only an appropriately polite response to the question, but it is a response that is true to me, my values and goals. I strive to live a simple life. The less mail (electronic or paper) I get the better. I also strive to live a financially secure life. So the fewer credit cards associated with my name the better.

I also live by the rule that you should only charge what you can pay for when the bill comes. If you can't afford to pay for it when the bill comes – you can't afford it.

If you wouldn't take out a loan at 15.90% to make a purchase, than you should only put it on your credit card if you will pay it off before interest is applied. A lot can happen in the 30 days between a purchase and when the bill comes. If you don't keep track it is easy to forget what you have charged. If you aren't sure what your balance is, log in and double check, or delay the purchase.

The Credit Trap

Payment Information

New Balance	$1,998.86
Minimum Payment Due	$39.00
Past Due Amount	$0.00
Payment Due Date	March 22, 2016

🕐 **Late Payment Warning:** If we do not receive your minimum payment by the date listed above, you may have to pay a late fee of up to $37 and your APRs may be increased to a Penalty APR of up to 28.49%.

The image above is a snap shot of the most critical section of my credit card statement. The **Late Payment Warning** section of this statement says it all. If my payment is late, I quickly get hit with a $37 late fee. That is $2 less than my minimum due! On top of it, the interest rate they charge me could be as high as 28.49%. So, a $100 purchase would become a purchase of

$128.49. If the roughly $2,000 goes unpaid for 12 months, I would owe **an additional $570 in interest alone.** Think of the fun weekend you could have with an extra $570. This extra amount quickly outweighs anything I would have "saved" by taking advantage of a "sale" on those killer heels or earning bonus points for opening a new credit account.

This is the trap. Your payment gets delayed or you don't pay the full amount, and the next thing you know your $2,000 balance becomes $2,500 because of added fees and interest. It can quickly get out of control! And, it continues to grow unless you start paying large amounts on the balance AND keep yourself from making additional purchases with the card.

Add to this the hit your credit score takes if the payment isn't on time, and the trap gets tighter. A $5,000 credit card balance with a 16% interest rate would take almost seven years to pay off with a monthly payment of $100.[1] This is how long it will take if you never add any other charges and assume no additional fees. The total interest paid would be over $3,000!

Don't get me wrong. Credit cards are a convenient way to pay. I don't go anywhere without one. Like a sharp knife it is a great tool, but if not used carefully it will cut you and leave you bleeding. Like the scar from a bad cut, the damage from credit card balances can take years, or even decades to fade away.

I only carry one credit card, and I pay off the full amount every month. As a result, I pay no interest. Plus, I earn credit card points that translate into a credit on my account in December of each year. Since I pay the full balance every month prior to the due date, the credit card company is essentially paying me to use the card! It is a great deal. However, it is only a good deal because there are no annual fees and I pay the balance in full each month prior to the due date.

How can they afford to pay me to use the card? They charge interchange fees to the retailers who accept the card as payment. Plus, they have a lot of customers who don't pay the full amount when due. Credit card issuers actually prefer customers who don't pay the full amount because they make a LOT of money off late fees and interest. They know that people like me who never pay credit card interest are less profitable for them than those paying interest on balances.

Interchange fees, also known as swipe fees, are charged to the merchant every time a credit card is used (swiped) at their location.[2] These fees get passed on to you through higher prices. The fees average over 2% per transaction and cost the average American family close to $400 per year, according to the National Retail Federation. Interchange fees also apply to transactions paid with most debit cards, although generally at a much lower rate, capped at $0.21 per transaction for most cards.

Credit card reward programs are designed to get more of your information and your money. The perceived value of the rewards helps motivate users to use their card(s). With each swipe, the card company receives a fee and information about your spending habits.

Be careful with the tricks of reward programs from retailers. These programs are tactics companies use to get you to spend more money.

Reward programs also allow the rewards company to gain personal information and data on your purchasing habits. This data can drive additional promotional offers, which drive additional purchases and additional fees.

In my experience, they usually have so many restrictions that whatever perks you get are usually worth far less than the effort they require on your part. They might change the rules or stop the program, which could happen at any time. And these days, they also pose a security risk. Unless it is your favorite place where you regularly shop, it is likely not worth your time or the risk.

I never make a purchase decision based on awards and points. If the item isn't worth the price I pay today without points, rewards, store bucks, credits, time sensitive gift cards or anything else, I will not buy it.

Loans

There are four primary components to a loan: principal, interest, collateral and fees. Principal is the term for the actual amount of money you borrow. Interest is the amount of money you are charged for borrowing the money until you pay it back. Collateral is the asset you are borrowing against. Fees are additional charges added to the loan to cover administrative costs. They are often called origination fees, points, or service fees, and they add up.

In the case of a car loan of $5,000, the principal is $5,000. The interest is the price of borrowing based on a percentage of the amount borrowed. Often what you are purchasing is used as the collateral. It is what the bank will repossess if you don't pay them back based on the terms of the loan, usually a car or a house. Loans with collateral are referred to as secured loans because there is something the bank can take back and resell. It provides the bank additional security to get their money back. This is why the bank holds the title to the car or house until the loan is paid.

Note I'm using the term bank here as a general term for any financial institution loaning money. It could be a credit union, an auto dealer, retailer, or other financial organization.

Since a pair of shoes, vacation or college degree can't be repossessed, loans for these items are considered unsecured because there is no collateral.

In this case, interest is the price you pay a bank or financial organization for letting you use their money. If you had the money to make the desired purchase, your purchase price is the cost of the item. If you don't have the money and instead take out a loan, the cost is the price plus interest, plus loan fees. If you are the person who is paying interest, you want the lowest interest rate possible. Here interest works against you because it increases your costs. In later chapters, we'll look at a way to have interest work for you by earning it instead of paying it.

The amortization schedule that follows shows the details of each loan payment for a $5,000 loan at 3% interest for three years (36 months). Looking at the first payment you will see that of the $145 paid, $133 is applied to the principal or the original amount of the loan. The remaining $12.50 is interest paid. The balance is what is left of the principal amount. This is the amount the interest is applied to for the next payment. Since the payment remains the same, the amount applied to the principal increases a little with each payment. Both the interest and the balance go down slightly with each payment. In the end, you would pay back the $5,000 plus $235 worth of interest for this loan.

Three percent interest is a very reasonable rate currently. The resulting interest for the entire three years is $235. Note that this example assumes no processing fees, origination fees, or other fees outside of the interest paid. But for someone with less than ideal credit, an interest rate of 7% is more likely. The total interest for the life of the loan at a 7% interest rate becomes $558 instead of $235.

A loan should only be used to purchase a long-term asset. Period. You should only loan money to get something you clearly need or will help you get ahead in life. A basic reliable car to get you to the better job, a small student loan to get you a program certificate at a local college, or a student loan to get you a professional job in a highly-paid field where there is market demand are a few examples. We'll talk more about assets in Chapter 10, but for now consider an asset something that has long-term value and will still have value after the loan is paid off.

Car Loan with Car as Collateral

Payment #	Amount	Principal	Interest	Balance
1	$145.41	$132.91	$12.50	$4,867.09
2	$145.41	$133.24	$12.17	$4,733.86
3	$145.41	$133.57	$11.83	$4,600.28
4	$145.41	$133.91	$11.50	$4,466.38
5	$145.41	$134.24	$11.17	$4,332.14
6	$145.41	$134.58	$10.83	$4,197.56
7	$145.41	$134.91	$10.49	$4,062.65
8	$145.41	$135.25	$10.16	$3,927.40
9	$145.41	$135.59	$9.82	$3,791.81
10	$145.41	$135.93	$9.48	$3,655.89
11	$145.41	$136.27	$9.14	$3,519.62
12	$145.41	$136.61	$8.80	$3,383.01
13	$145.41	$136.95	$8.46	$3,246.07
14	$145.41	$137.29	$8.12	$3,108.77
15	$145.41	$137.63	$7.77	$2,971.14
16	$145.41	$137.98	$7.43	$2,833.16
17	$145.41	$138.32	$7.08	$2,694.84
18	$145.41	$138.67	$6.74	$2,556.17
19	$145.41	$139.02	$6.39	$2,417.15
20	$145.41	$139.36	$6.04	$2,277.79
21	$145.41	$139.71	$5.69	$2,138.08
22	$145.41	$140.06	$5.35	$1,998.02
23	$145.41	$140.41	$5.00	$1,857.61
24	$145.41	$140.76	$4.64	$1,716.85
25	$145.41	$141.11	$4.29	$1,575.73
26	$145.41	$141.47	$3.94	$1,434.27
27	$145.41	$141.82	$3.59	$1,292.45
28	$145.41	$142.17	$3.23	$1,150.27
29	$145.41	$142.53	$2.88	$1,007.74
30	$145.41	$142.89	$2.52	$864.85
31	$145.41	$143.24	$2.16	$721.61
32	$145.41	$143.60	$1.80	$578.01
33	$145.41	$143.96	$1.45	$434.05
34	$145.41	$144.32	$1.09	$289.73
35	$145.41	$144.68	$0.72	$145.04
36	$145.41	$145.04	$0.36	$0.00
Total	$5,234.76	$5,000.00	$234.63	

Credit Score = Your Financial Reputation

Like your personal reputation, your financial reputation takes years to establish and only minutes to destroy. Fortunately, unlike your personal reputation, credit scores are based on a math-driven formula that has no tie to your friend's credit score. As long as you pay the bill, what you did in Vegas stays in Vegas. But if you don't pay the bill, future creditors and future employers will find out when they check your credit.

Having no credit history is far better than having a bad credit history. People and firms are willing to take a small risk on someone who hasn't yet established a credit history. But if they see you have a history of not paying your obligations, they are far less likely to trust you and extend you credit or a job offer.

There are a variety of credit scores used by prospective creditors, employers, and insurance carriers. The FICO (Fair, Isaac, and Company) score is the most common. It is based on credit files from the three national credit bureaus: Experian, Equifax, and TransUnion.[3] Because data collected by each bureau varies, your credit score could vary based on the credit bureau used, although the resulting scores are generally very similar.

Credit Score Scale	
Excellent	800 - 850
Above Average	740 - 799
Average	670 - 739
Below Average	580 - 669
Poor	300 - 579

The higher your score, the better off you'll be. A higher score makes it more likely you will be approved for a loan and at a lower interest rate. With a higher score, it's easier to rent an apartment and get a job.

Yes, many employers are using credit scores in hiring decisions. They do this because there is statistical evidence that shows people with high credit scores are more reliable. As a result, they tend to be dependable and more stable employees.

Credit scores or a variation of them are also used in insurance policy pricing. Someone with an above average credit score of 775, for example, will pay significantly less for auto insurance then a person with a score of 650. The exact same coverage and policy is cheaper for the girl with the higher score. Why? Statistically, those with higher credit scores have fewer claims. This is one of the few things in life that rewards those who do the right thing. Pay your bills on time, don't buy more than what you can afford, and you'll be rewarded with lower interest rates, lower insurance rates, and more opportunities.

All other factors being the same, those with high scores will pay significantly less over the life of their loan. On a four-year used car loan of $10,000, a three-point difference in interest rate results in an additional $652. Just think what you could do with an additional $652 dollars. That could buy a lot of shoes. So, it truly pays to pay attention to your credit score. But how do you do it?

The following pie chart shows how much of your total score is determined by each credit factor.[4] These factors are important to know, but you should also keep them in perspective. If you manage your credit, your score will reflect it. But it is not a full picture of your financial well-being, so don't obsess over it unless your score is below 700. If it is below 700, it is worth dedicated attention to keep moving it up.

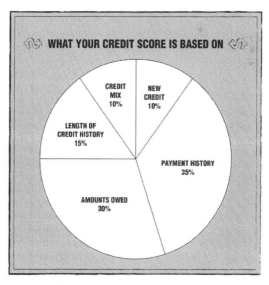

WHAT YOUR CREDIT SCORE IS BASED ON

CREDIT MIX 10%
NEW CREDIT 10%
LENGTH OF CREDIT HISTORY 15%
PAYMENT HISTORY 35%
AMOUNTS OWED 30%

59

Payment History makes up 35% of your score. Pay your bills on time or early and you are half-way there. Payment history is the biggest part so I emphasize the importance of this factor for a reason. This takes into consideration whether you pay your bills at all and if you pay them on time. These are accounts like credit cards, car loans, store credit cards (local furniture stores), mortgages, etc.

Fortunately, not all late payments are the same. The score calculations take in to consideration how many days late a payment is made (30, 60, 90 days or more), how much is owed, how recently you paid late, and how many accounts have delinquent payments.

According to the *Frequently Asked Questions About FICO Scores* document provided by FICO, **a 30-day delinquent payment can reduce a credit score by 60 to 110 points.**[5] Failing to pay one bill for 30 days could make the difference between getting a loan, a rental unit, or even a job. The higher your score, the more you have to lose; higher scores take a bigger hit.

Public record events such as bankruptcies, foreclosures, wage attachments, liens, and judgments are all considered serious and will weigh heavily on your score. The more recent they are, the bigger impact they have on your score. These items generally stay on your credit record for seven years.

Amounts Owed is another large factor in the credit score calculation. This factor looks at how much you owe compared to the total amount of credit you have. For example, a $50 balance on a credit card with a $10,000 limit is a better ratio than a $9,500 balance on the same credit card. A low balance with a high limit shows creditors are willing to give you more credit than you generally use. The closer your balance is to your credit limit, the riskier you look to a creditor.

Of course, not all accounts and loans are treated the same. Car loans and home mortgages are generally expected to have higher balances. With these loans, they look to see how much the original loan amount was compared to what is currently

owed on it. They want to see that the amount owed has gradually gone down the longer you've had the loan.

Length of Credit History is 15% of your score. It considers
how long you have had credit and how recently you have used
your credit accounts. The longer your credit history, the better
off your credit score will be. This is one case where time and
age can be on your side.

Credit Mix in Use looks at the mix of your different credit accounts. You don't need to have one of every type of account
(revolving, retail, auto loan, installment and mortgage), but
having only revolving or retail accounts may be a red flag for
some creditors. In the end, this only makes up 10% of your
score. Even if your credit accounts are all retail and credit
cards, paying your bills on time is more important than having
a variety of accounts.

New Credit is only 10% of your total credit score. Research
shows that those who open multiple accounts in a short period of time are a greater credit risk. It can be a sign of financial troubles. It is best to take out a little credit at a time over
multiple years than to take it out all at once or all around the
same time.

Because credit scores are so important, all U.S. residents are
allowed one free credit report from each of the three credit
bureaus each year. Take advantage of this and request yours.
To do this go to www.annualcreditreport.com or call
1-877-322-8228.[6] This site will not provide your actual credit
score, but you can see the underlying history on which your
score is based (and you can pay to see the score, if you wish).
If your accounts are in good order and you don't have delinquent or late payments, your score should be fine.

If you have concerns about identity theft, you could order a
free report from a different bureau every four months to stay
on top of it and detect any identity theft or errors.

Many credit card companies are now providing customers
their credit score for free with their monthly statements. This

is a nice perk, so it is worth asking about if you don't see it on your monthly statement or when you login to your account. Some credit card companies are even offering it free to non-customers. There are also countless credit services and identity theft services that are willing to provide you your credit score for a fee. Make sure they are reputable before you share your personal information.

How to Establish Credit

Now that you understand credit and credit scores, here are some tips for establishing credit without getting sucked into the credit trap. The best way to establish credit is slowly and carefully. Establish credit accounts or take out loans as you need them over time, and have the financial capacity to pay them off.

You shouldn't jump into the deep-end of the pool until you are a proven swimmer. Trust me, I tried this once when I was 5 years old. The cool teenager I was trying to impress had to save me, and I promptly threw-up on the pool deck while everyone watched.

Like jumping into the deep-end of the pool, taking on too much credit all at once can quickly get out of hand. Instead of looking cool, you could look like the young fool. You'll be much better off building your strength in the shallow-end first.

There are a lot of ways to build credit. Having a general-purpose credit card with no balances is a good example. I like having one major credit card that is widely accepted at local, national and international locations. It should only be used for purchases you would be buying with cash or a check (meaning you have the money already) so you can comfortably pay in full when the bill comes due.

Establishing credit is really about establishing a positive habit. Your habit should be to pay the bill in full and on-time every month. Paying in full means paying the total balance—NOT just the minimum amount. Your habit should also be to pay a week in advance if sending by mail or two days in advance if paying online. This may be a little old-fashioned, but mail still gets delayed and computer glitches happen. You can always kill time if you show up early, but if you show up late you can't get back the lost time.

Chapter 7
Where to Keep Your Money

The best way to predict the future is to create it.

Abraham Lincoln

Account Purpose Determines Account Type

Organizing your money isn't much different from organizing your closet. You want the clothing you wear on a regular basis in the front where you can easily grab it. The formal dress you wear once a year is off to the side or in the back.

The key to deciding where to put your money is to match the purpose of the money to the function of the account. Standard checking and savings accounts are perfect for the everyday and periodic expenses and savings. Money for the mid-term savings, like a car or home, can be in a standard savings account, but is better kept in a certificate of deposit (CD) or a low-risk mutual fund where it is safe and can potentially gain interest to keep up with inflation. These types of accounts are also good for emergency accounts. Long term savings (around 10 years or longer) and retirement funds should go into more aggressive mutual funds.

The money you use for daily living and monthly or regular expenses should be somewhere easy to access. Your regular savings for incidentals and planned expenses should be somewhere easy to access, and today's technology makes this easy with most accounts. When I refer to easy access here, I am more focused on the mental energy it takes for you to keep track of it. There is also the convenience of being able to stop by a local branch or find an ATM to consider.

To keep it simple, my regular checking and savings accounts are in the same bank and tied to each other. I can easily transfer money between the two as needed. I can log into one website and see all accounts with a click of a button.

My mid- to long-range saving accounts are held with a mutual fund company that also has my retirement account. These are low transaction accounts. These funds are invested in the stock market, and are best kept where I don't see them every day. If I checked on them every few days, I would go insane from watching the ups and downs of the market. It is also best for them to be with a strong company with low fees.

Account Type

Checking Account: This is the account type you use to pay all of your bills. It is where you direct deposit or automatically transfer the amount of your expected expenses for the pay period. Remember, the remainder goes into your general savings account.

Checking accounts are designed for frequent transactions, with money regularly coming in and out. As a result, they generally pay little, if any, interest. Since they are high volume transaction accounts, there are often fees associated with them. Talk to your bank or credit union to find the lowest fee account that meets your needs.

General Savings Account: This is where the rest of your paycheck goes. You could also call it near-term savings. If expenses are a little higher one month, you transfer from your general savings to your checking. I recommend maintaining a balance between $2,000 and $4,000. This extra cash is there for the expensive incidental expenses that always happen such as replacement tires, major auto repair, or moving costs and first month's rent and deposit. When this account reaches a comfortable balance, you can start focusing on your emergency savings.

Certificate of Deposit (CD): CDs are low-risk deposit accounts. They have a set interest rate based on the amount you deposit and the predetermined length of time you will keep the money deposited. Term lengths are generally 6 months to 5 years.

Money Market accounts: These accounts are like a hybrid between a checking account and a savings account. Think of them as a low transaction volume checking account. They generally require a higher minimum balance in exchange for earning a little interest.

Mutual Funds: Mutual Funds are investment accounts, and we cover these in Chapter 16: Investing Terms You Need to Know.

Every bank is different and financial organizations regularly update their account terms, so you'll want to read your account information and know what fees and penalties apply. With all of these accounts, make sure you are in the lowest fee structure possible. You don't want your savings to be eaten up with fees you can avoid.

Account Purpose

Emergency Fund: The purpose behind an emergency fund is that it only gets used for a true emergency – an unexpected job loss or a natural disaster. This means it should be rare, if ever, you need to use it! You want to have three to six months of expenses saved. In Chapter 8, you'll determine in detail what your living expenses are and how much you would need to save for an emergency.

I recommend having at least three months of expenses in an account that is easy to access. This would be a basic savings account or a money market account. If you needed the money tomorrow, you could get it without worry that the stock market is down. The more you have in the account, the more appealing a CD becomes. The downside of a CD is if you do find yourself in an emergency situation and you take out the money prior to its maturity date, you lose some or all of the expected interest for the period. This can be a risk worth taking in exchange for some interest.

Mid-Term or Special Purpose Savings: This account is for your bigger goals and expenses. A car, college courses, a wedding, or a down payment for a home would fit into this category. A general savings account is good for these funds. If you are a disciplined saver and your time line for using the money is relatively short (0-3 years), you can use your general savings account to park this money. I prefer having a separate account because it is easier to keep track of where I am compared to my goal. Plus, I am not as tempted to spend it as I might be if it were sitting in my regular savings account.

If your goal is further out (5-10 years) a balanced mutual fund or long-term CDs are a better location for it. They have more risk but may be offset by the upside potential. A balanced mutual fund is one that has a mix of both conservative low risk bonds and higher risk stocks.

Retirement Accounts: These accounts have the longest time line and should take advantage of the tax regulations that allow for tax-deferred growth. Put as much as you can (up to the maximum contribution limits) into these accounts while you are young and working so you can have a comfortable retirement later in life. Retirement accounts are covered in more detail in Chapter 15.

Long-Term Investing: If you are a rock star saver and have already maxed out your retirement account, investing in a low cost mutual fund like an index fund is a great way to go to save additional money for the long term.

The Go To Hell Fund: It's About Having Options

As I mentioned in the Preface, my mother wished she had enough money to allow her to say "Go to hell" to those who mistreated her and still pay the bills, regardless of their reaction. Having a Go To Hell fund is as much about having options as it is about having money. It's about being able to walk out if someone pushes you up against the wall, and still have the comfort of knowing you can make rent next week.

A GTH is not about being rude, disrespectful, or throwing a dramatic temper tantrum. It's about not feeling trapped in a situation you think you can't afford to leave. It is about having a safety net that allows you to take a risk you would otherwise be too scared to take.

It could be called the "I have choices fund." Once while listening to a radio program, I heard one of the richest women in the world say she has money set aside in case all her businesses and professional operations fail. She calls it the homeless fund. It is her safety net fund that will keep her from becoming homeless if everything else in her life falls apart. You can call it whatever you want. If you aren't being treated with the respect you deserve and you need to change your situation, having this money can make the leap a little less scary, or the landing after a fall a little softer.

Regardless of what you call it, having a back-up/plan B/GTH fund can not only give you the practical dollars to take the risk, but it helps give you that extra ounce of confidence you need. It's the peace of mind that says if plan A doesn't work, I have something to fall back on, something to keep me going.

Some might confuse a GTH fund with an emergency fund. Since a GTH fund is simply a name you give to the money you have set aside, any or all of the account types we've covered could work. Which accounts to use depend on the purpose — whom you want to tell to GTH.

For some, the GTH fund might be used to put distance between you and overbearing parents. For others, the GTH fund is for ditching a boss. Freedom from overbearing or controlling parents can be taken care of with a checking account, a savings account, and a job. Ditching the boss will require a lot more money, so it would likely include all the above accounts to be in place and well supplied. Spoiler Alert:

If you want to quit your job before having a new one, you'll need the equivalent of your paycheck for 6-12 months, depending on the job market in your field in the area you want to work.

If you are sick of having a roommate and you want the freedom to live alone, you need enough income or savings to pay the rent and extra utilities. If rent is $1,000 and you currently pay half, you are looking at an additional $6,000 a year for the luxury to have the place to yourself.

It can be fun to think about how you would tell the boss you quit or the roommate you are leaving. It's like fantasizing about what you would do if you won the lottery. Some of these scenarios would sound a lot like the classic country song "Take this Job and Shove It," by Johnny Paycheck.[1] His stage name alone says a lot.

The reality is usually much less dramatic, but the feeling of satisfaction is the same. You hold your head a little higher. You have a little more confidence in your stride. And it could be weeks before you shake off the gleeful smile.

The name and how I think about this savings has changed over time. My motivation has shifted from wanting to tell someone else where to go, to telling a friend where I plan to go. In midlife, I now think of being able to tell a friend I'm going to spend months or even years in one of my favorite countries with my husband. The savings is the same, but what motivates me has changed as my life has changed. The more I save, the more ideas I come up with to do with the savings.

Chapter 8
Budget to Know Where You Are

Don't tell me what your priorities are.
Show me your budget and I'll tell you what your
priorities are.

Vice President Joe Biden

Mental Map for Your Money

If you wouldn't manage your time without a calendar or clock, then you shouldn't manage your money without a budget.

The term budget has gotten a bad reputation, as if it were a complicated 10-page book report on every dollar you make and spend. It isn't! It is a priority list for your money. It will reflect the value you put on education, housing, material possessions, entertainment, transportation, charity, shoes, and pretty much everything in life. While there are certainly things outside of your control, we all have choices we make every day. And those choices reflect our values. If you are spending money, it is safe to say you value what you are spending money on at some level. Otherwise, you shouldn't be spending money on it. Right?

A budget is also more about planning than it is about math. It can be as detailed as you like. It just has to be realistic. It needs to capture your expenses. It also requires you to be honest with yourself and those around you. Those who avoid doing a budget will use time or math as an excuse. In truth, it is usually their desire to avoid the reality of their choices they have been making that keeps them from looking at their spending.

There are generally three versions of your budget. The first is what you _think_ your budget is. The second is what it _actually_ is. The third is what you _want_ it to be.

Start with what you think your budget is. Using a blank piece of paper, write down your best estimate of what your monthly income is. Then jot down all your expenses each month. You don't have to spend a lot of time on this one. Just put down your best estimate. This shouldn't take more than a couple of minutes. The point is to take a high level look at your income and expenses.

After you have listed all your expenses, add them up and compare them to your income to get a rough idea of your bottom line. Is the result a positive number or a negative number? Here I am, using the math terms positive and negative. Yet, the real life meaning and impact are obvious. You can't regularly spend more than you earn without experiencing negative consequences.

Now that you have a rough idea in your head around your spending, it is time to look at your actual spending. **A budget is like a map. It will show you how to get somewhere but you first have to know where you are.** To do that, you need to take a close look at your actual income and expenses. You need to do this part; anyone who has ever gotten lost can tell you the problem usually starts because you aren't where you think you are.

Actual Budget

This next step will point to exactly where you are financially. The "Your Actual Budget" (where you are now) form will help you determine where you are financially right now. An electronic spreadsheet is available for you online at AGirlsGuidetoFinance.com if you prefer to do it electronically. A copy is also available in Chapter 22: Tools and Resources.

Your Actual Budget (where you are now)

Monthly Income & Deductions	
	Gross Income (before taxes and deductions)
	- Pre-tax Retirement Savings (i.e., traditional 401(k))
	- Health Insurance and other pre-tax deductions
	Subtotal (pre-tax)
	- After-tax Retirement Savings (i.e., Roth 401(k))
	- Taxes
	- After-tax deductions
	Net Monthly Income (net pay x paychecks per month)
Monthly Expenses	
Housing	
	Rent/Mortgage
	Utilities (water, electric, heating, trash, etc.)
	Phone
	Cable, internet, etc.
	Insurance
Transportation	
	Car/Transportation (car, bus, train, Uber)
	Car Insurance (annual premium divided by 12)
	Gas & Maintenance
Debt/Loans	
	Student Loans (total monthly payment of all loans)
	Credit Card Debt (Any balance over 30 days old)
	Personal Loans or Retail Debt
General Living	
	Groceries & Home Essentials
	Medical (Rx, co-pays, wellness items)
	Clothing
	General Living/Miscellaneous
Non-essentials	
	Entertainment (eating out, girls' night, movies)
	Charity
	Miscellaneous (gifts, Girl Scout cookies, just because)
Savings	
	Life Happens Fund
	Emergency Fund then to Debt Reduction
	Mid and Long-term Goals (grad school, vehicle, etc.)
	Total Monthly Expenses
	Gain or Loss

The first step to understanding where you are on your financial map is to determine your monthly net pay. The form has room to include all the figures that determine your net pay, but for this exercise you could go straight to net pay. To do this, find your net pay amount on your pay stub. For Ashley, this was line 20 of the pay stub we saw in Chapter 5. Now, multiply your net pay amount by the number of times you get paid each month. Ashley is paid twice a month so for her it would be $1124.56 x 2 = $2,249.12. This amount goes into the Net Monthly Income spot (last row in the income section) under monthly income.

If you have two jobs, make sure you include net income from both. If your income varies from month-to-month, use an average. If you are married and share the income and expenses, include amounts from all sources. Do the same with all expenses.

For the purposes of this exercise, we're assuming you are either a salaried employee or work predictable and regular hours such that the net amount each pay period is a relatively stable amount.

If that is not the case and your income is unpredictable because your income is based off commission, you do freelance work, or have a seasonal job, I recommend you set your budget based on the lowest expected income. Any earnings above your budgeted minimum amount can be applied to savings. This way you structure your budget so you minimally meet your obligations.

Now, take out your bills and write in all the amounts you paid for expenses. Remember to add up all your utility expenses, all the gas station stops, and any maintenance expenses. Do the same with all of the eating out expenses and grocery store stops, entertainment, etc.

If you are like most, you'll end up with a lot of miscellaneous expenses or ATM withdrawals. You will likely find it is hard to account for all the money that you spent. That's okay. This exercise is meant to increase your awareness of your spending. Your desired budget will be far more accurate. You'll be more likely to follow it if you are clear about what you *have* been spending and not just about what you *want* to be spending.

KEEPING WHAT YOU EARN

Here, you need to take an honest look at what you actually spent last month, and the month or two before that. If you spent $1,000 eating out, you need to be honest with yourself about it. You don't have to have a record of every $5 purchase, but you do need to pull out (or access online) all of your bills, account statements, and credit and debit card statements so you can see where and how much you are spending. You will likely see little amounts quickly add up.

It is hard to categorize all of your spending into just a few categories. But it does allow us to simplify our thinking and focus on the big picture. Here is a breakdown of spending categories.

Housing – In this category, you want to include all the expenses associated with keeping a roof over your head. That will include things like rent or mortgage payments, insurance, utilities, water, etc.

Transportation – This category is for all the expenses associated with getting where you need to go. For many, these expenses are associated with vehicle ownership, like a car payment, insurance, gas, maintenance, and parking expenses. For others, it will include train or subway fare, cabs, Uber or Lyft expenses, and other costs associated with getting you where you need to go.

Debt – Debt can include credit card balances or loans that aren't already captured under housing and transportation. Common debt expenses include student loans, credit card balances, store purchases that have been financed (like appliances and furniture), and home equity lines of credit.

General Living – Here, you want to include all the other expenses needed in life. Food and clothing are the obvious expenses, but these days computer and internet would be considered by many as living essentials. This would also include medical expenses that aren't covered by insurance like co-payments for prescription drugs and fitness club memberships to stay in shape. I also include home essentials like toilet paper, light bulbs and detergent.

Nonessentials – As the label suggests, these are the expenses that are not required in day-to-day living, but most of us incur. They include entertainment, hobbies, eating out, gift giving, and other expenses that don't fit into the other categories. I also put charitable giving in this category, not because I don't consider giving essential, but because this category is about optional spending. If your paycheck is short this month or you have an unexpected medical bill, you could give up the nonessentials for a month or two to get back on track.

Saving – Just like there are multiple expense categories, there are multiple savings categories. There are the basic incidentals of life like Christmas gifts; a friend's wedding or life happens stuff; true emergencies; and mid-term and long-term savings. If you are contributing to an employer sponsored retirement plan (like a 401(k) plan) that has already been subtracted from your pay, do not include it here since it has already been taken out. Money you put into an IRA should be included under savings mid- and long-term goals.

These categories fit 90% of the average person's expenses, but this is your budget so make it fit you. Add or subtract categories to best fit your spending. If you want to capture every cent and have 30 categories, go for it. If you are happy rounding up spending and creating three categories, (i.e., must have, want to have and dream of having), that's great, too. You do you.

Here again, the categories and the math are just about keeping score so you know where you stand. They help you compare and plan for where you want to be in the future.

What matters is the meaning the categories hold for you. It is the meaning and value you put on them that is important, because it is the personal meaning that will drive your behavior. It is about establishing the habit of evaluating and making financial decisions based on your priorities. Once you have the habit, the details can adjust as you grow and experience different situations.

entertainment	$12.99
gas	$10.75
family phone	$291.61
gas	$16.01
food	$18.62
entertainment	$2.99
health/fitness	$80.50
car	$11.00
groceries	$21.20
entertainment	$24.00
parking/car	$4.25
clothing	$31.80
gas	$14.43
car	$464.50
food	$9.81
parking/car	$3.00
insurance	$16.90
gas	$14.99
utility	$95.00
clothing/makeup	$68.69
entertainment	$3.96
groceries	$84.78

This snapshot was taken of my credit card bill. I went through each purchase and identified each by spending category.

As you can see, I spent a lot on clothing, make-up, and car related items that month. That is unusual for me, but I went on a road trip vacation that month. The month prior, I didn't spend anything on clothing and only $50 on transportation, so I will average them out to estimate my actual monthly spending.

Once you have written down all of your expenses, take a minute to review them. Are you spending more than you thought you were? Are you spending too much in one area but not enough in another? Most importantly, is your actual spending in line with what you value?

Too often we find ourselves spending money on things our friends and family value more than we do. Everyone has an opinion on how we should and shouldn't spend our money. It is good to listen to others and gain their insight but if it isn't something you value, ask yourself this: why are you spending your hard-earned money on it?

Desired Budget

Now that you have a clear picture on what you have been spending, it is time to decide what you value and where you really want to spend your money.

Budget Guidelines	
Category	% of Income
Housing	20-35%
Transportation	10-15%
Debt/Loans	0-20%
General Living	20-40%
Nonessentials	5-20%
Savings	10-50%

Here are some guidelines to keep in mind as you work on your budget going forward. If your actual spending on any category is greater than the guideline percentages, I recommend you evaluate your expenses for that category.

In Your Desired Monthly Budget form, enter what you want your spending to be. If you increase your spending in one category, you need to reduce it in another category. Your total monthly expenses need to be less than your monthly net pay. You may run into a month where this isn't the case, but this should not be reflected in your desired budget.

The advantage of using a spreadsheet for your budget is you can quickly modify and adjust your spending projections and see the impact it has on your spending plan. You can play with ideas like getting a roommate to share housing expenses and see how it impacts what you can save. You can see how reducing your debt can increase your savings and spending. Or, how a second job can super-charge your savings or cover your car payment. The more you understand your expenses, the more you can control them.

Living on a budget isn't about tracking every expense and feeling like you can't afford anything; it is about reflecting your true self through your pocket book. It is about reflecting your priorities in your day-to-day choices.

Your Desired Monthly Budget

Monthly Income & Deductions	
	Gross Income (before taxes and deductions)
	- Pre-tax Retirement Savings (i.e., traditional 401(k))
	- Health Insurance and other pre-tax deductions
	Subtotal (pre-tax)
	- After-tax Retirement Savings (i.e., Roth 401(k))
	- Taxes
	- After-tax deductions
	Net Monthly Income (net pay x paychecks per month)
Monthly Expenses	
Housing (20 - 35%)	
	Rent/Mortgage
	Utilities (water, electric, heating, trash, etc.)
	Phone
	Cable, internet, etc.
	Insurance
Transportation (10-15%)	
	Car/Transportation (car, bus, train, Uber)
	Car Insurance (annual premium divided by 12)
	Gas & Maintenance
Debt/Loans (0-20%)	
	Student Loans (total monthly payment of all loans)
	Credit Card Debt (Any balance over 30 days old)
	Personal Loans or Retail Debt
General Living (20-40%)	
	Groceries & Home Essentials
	Medical (Rx, co-pays, wellness items)
	Clothing
	General Living/Miscellaneous
Non-essentials (5-20%)	
	Entertainment (eating out, girls' night, movies)
	Charity
	Miscellaneous (gifts, Girl Scout cookies, just because)
Savings (10-50%)	
	Life Happens Fund **Bare Minimum $25**
	Emergency Fund then to Debt Reduction
	Mid and Long-term Goals (grad school, vehicle, etc.)
	Total Monthly Expenses
	Gain or Loss

In your 20s and 30s, debt reduction may be your priority. In your 40s and 50s, saving may be your priority. In your 60s and 70s, giving to others and/or living out a dream may be your priority. Your priorities may change, but the same good habits will get you through all phases of life.

Of course, the reverse is also true. If you have poor spending and budgeting habits, those could have a negative impact throughout your life.

Now that Ashley has a job, she wants to find an apartment and live on her own. To help determine how much she can spend on rent, she writes down her income and her monthly expenses. With a clear understanding of her income and her set expenses Ashley created her desired monthly budget.

For Ashley, going to grad school without increasing her student loans is a priority. She can accomplish this goal by getting a roommate and taking night classes while she works.

She's hoping to save a few dollars each month on food, entertainment and misc. expenses to give her a little more cushion and savings. She knows keeping within her budget will be tricky. However, if she builds the habit now, any raise she receives or expenses she cuts will go directly to improving her bottom line.

Ashley's Desired Monthly Budget

Monthly & Income Deductions

$3,462	Gross Income (before taxes and deductions)
$208	- Pre-tax Retirement Savings (i.e., traditional 401(k))
$210	- Health Insurance and other pre-tax deductions
$3,044	Subtotal (pre-tax)
$0	- After-tax Retirement Savings (i.e., Roth 401(k))
$775	- Taxes
$20	- After-tax deductions
$2,249	Net Monthly Income (net pay x paychecks per month)

Monthly Expenses

Housing (20 - 35%)

$550	Rent/Mortgage
$75	Utilities (water, electric, heating, trash, etc.)
$75	Phone
$80	Cable, internet, etc.
$5	Insurance

Transportation (10-15%)

$245	Car/Transportation (car, bus, train, Uber)
$35	Car Insurance (annual premium divided by 12)
$60	Gas $40 & Maintenance $20

Debt/Loans (0-20%)

$300	Student Loans (total monthly payment of all loans)
$0	Credit Card Debt (Any balance over 30 days old)
$0	Personal Loans or Retail Debt

General Living (20-40%)

$325	Groceries & Home Essentials
$30	Medical (Rx, co-pays, wellness items)
$50	Clothing
$35	General Living/Miscellaneous

Non-essentials (5-20%)

$50	Entertainment (eating out, girls' night, movies)
$40	Charity
$20	Miscellaneous (gifts, Girl Scout cookies, just because)

Savings (10-50%)

$70	Life Happens Fund **Bare Minimum $25**
$200	Emergency Fund then to Debt Reduction & Long-term Goals
$0	Mid and Long-term Goals (grad school, investing, etc.)
$2,245	**Total Monthly Expenses**

$ 4	Gain	**Positive Balance = WINNING!**

Like Ashley and everyone who has managed on a budget, you learn each month is a little different. Some expenses are very predictable (rent, cable bill, car payment). Other expenses vary from month to month. You may go two months without buying any clothes, but once a season you make a few wardrobe additions and spend three month's worth of your clothing budget in one shopping trip. That's fine as long as your monthly spending isn't more than your monthly budget you are good.

In Ashley's case she doesn't shop much and likes to do it in the shops near her hometown. She doesn't go every month, so it isn't uncommon for her to spend zero on clothing in January and $100 in February. As long as her total in two months isn't over her two-month budget, she is fine.

Of course, that assumes her total spending in any one month doesn't exceed her planned monthly expenses. In Ashley's case, she allows herself $50 for clothing, $50 for entertainment and $20 for miscellaneous expenses. She knows if she overspends on clothing she must underspend on entertainment and/or miscellaneous that month. Ashley considers these three categories discretionary. She allows herself flexibility between these categories as long as she doesn't spend more than the combined total of all three.

Variation from month to month happens. It is another reason why setting your expenses to a specified amount helps keep these variations from eating away at your savings. If it was in your budget last month but you didn't spend it, the money should be sitting in your account for you to spend this month.

For example, Ashley had a big project at work last week and then went home to visit family two of the four weekends of the previous month. As a result, she only spent half of her entertainment budget. This means that next month she doesn't have to worry if she takes in an extra show.

You may be surprised at how freeing it is when you cap your spending. As long as you pay for your set expenses, you have the flexibility to spend as you please up to that limit.

Like any new habit, it may feel uncomfortable at first. But once it is an established habit you won't even think about it. It will be like brushing your teeth each morning; you do it because failing to do it would feel awkward. Every time you come in under budget, you not only have the reward of extra money in the bank but the satisfaction that comes with having control over an important part of your life.

Chapter 9
Shop Smart

*The most alluring thing
a woman can have is confidence.*

Beyoncé

Everyone is fighting for your money. You should too.

Your job is to work as hard to keep your money as marketers work to get your money. The job of an ad, commercial, or sales person is to get you to visualize how great you'll look and feel in the blouse, car, loft or whatever they are trying to sell. This chapter points out some of the common tricks used to get you to buy, buy now, and buy more. I am sure you can identify even more on your own; they are everywhere.

Knowing and being aware of sales tactics commonly used against you will help you evaluate potential purchases. That way your spending decisions are based on your values, priorities, and needs, *not* on the goals of a retailer trying to move inventory.

Know the real cost

It has become harder and harder to know the real cost of what you are purchasing. Pay attention to the cash register. So many dollars are lost at the point of sale by error, by misleading sales signs, misunderstanding, or cash register coding issue. If it is important enough to buy, it is important enough to pay attention to the actual price at purchase. At many retailers, cash registers don't display the itemized amounts of your purchase. At many retailers, you are lucky if your total purchased amount is displayed at all, let alone the cost of each item. This makes it hard, if not impossible, to see if it rang up correctly. Did you get the discount you were expecting? Is the number of items correct?

Add to this all the clerk questions and check out distractions, and it is almost impossible to pay attention to the register as it rings up your purchase. Would you like to use your store credit card, would you like another item for half off, can I have your email address, would you like to donate a $1 to charity? These are just a few of the questions store clerks ask to add to your current or future purchases.

Since most purchases are transacted with the swipe of a card, it is easy to lose track of the amount you are spending. This is why some advise to only pay with cash. It is harder to overspend with cash. You have to physically pull it out of your wallet and hand it to someone; how much you have left becomes VERY obvious.

For me, carrying cash for all my spending isn't practical for my lifestyle. As a busy working mom, I have limited time to shop for family essentials so I need to get in and out fast. Debt cards work best. Like cash, the money is taken directly out of my account. I started doing this before mobile banking existed, so I had to mentally track my spending. I had a set spending amount for living expenses. As long as I stayed under that amount each pay period, I was good. Mobile banking has made tracking expenses easier, but it is still up to you to factor in the spending you have to do in the coming days.

Don't Let a Penny Change Your Mind

For some reason, we humans are more comfortable spending $14.99 than spending $15.00, despite that it is only a 1-cent difference. In our minds, it feels far less. Marketers for virtually every product from candy to cars take advantage of this fact. Part of this may be because it makes the math seem harder and they hope you don't do the math. Most people these days would not bend over to pick up a penny if they found one on the ground but are willing to let that same penny influence a $49.99 buying decision. It sounds crazy but we all do it.

Do yourself a favor. Round up, and then ask yourself if it is worth it.

Another marketing trick is to emphasize the amount you save and not the amount you pay. SAVE **$20.00** is proclaimed big and bold on the sign. For those like me who rush through the store (or web site) in a hurry, all you see as you scan the rack is **$20.00**. It's not until you pay at the register that you figure out the price you pay is actually $89.99. By this point you have your heart set on it and are flustered by the surprise and higher cost, so you go ahead and swipe your card.

This has happened to me many times. Sometimes I roll with it and buy the item anyway. More and more I have gotten comfortable with politely saying to the clerk, "I'm sorry but I misunderstood the price and I no longer want to buy it. Will you please take that item off?"

Even when I carefully read the sales sign and follow the qualifiers, it still happens. While Christmas shopping one year, I was picking up some dress socks as a gift. Boring, I know, but it was what my husband wanted. The sign on the rack said 3 for $30. I carefully selected three from the rack and made sure they were all the same brand. I had other items and hadn't kept track of my total. When the clerk rang it up and gave me the total I was surprised. I wasn't sure what it should be and couldn't see the prices on the register, so I asked him to tell me the prices of the items. Sure enough, the 3 for $30 had some odd exception not noted on the sign. Most of the socks were actually $17 instead of $10. When the clerk saw my frustration, he apologized if the sign was misleading and adjusted the price to match the sign.

Looking Good Doesn't Have to Cost a Lot

Having a Burberry purse may look cool to the five percent of the people in the world who can tell the difference between an authentic Burberry clutch and a knock-off, but you will feel like a fake if you have no money to put in it. It is FAR better to have someone pay attention to who you are or what you say than to have them pay attention to you because of the bag you use to carry your cell phone and other essentials.

We've all seen the girl who wears all the latest designer fashion and accessories so people will notice, but all you see is the fashion, not the person. There is nothing wrong with designer merchandise; you just need to be clear on what it does and doesn't provide you. A designer purse provides you a bag to carry your wallet and sun-glasses, but it will not fill your wallet or attract true friends. If you like it and can afford it, great! But if you are wearing it for any other reason, you should consider what that reason is and be clear about it. The price of your purse has nothing to do with your value or your worth.

There are some items where high quality is worth the extra cost, but more often than not, looking good doesn't have to cost a lot. You don't have to be a country music fan to appreciate the great wisdom in the Gretchen Wilson song, "Redneck Women." The lyrics make the point a girl can look just as nice in an outfit at half price.[1]

What looks good on someone has more to do with the color, style and how the person feels in it than anything else. We've all spent too much on heels or a strapless dress for a special occasion, only to be miserable all night. How much you spend on an outfit doesn't determine how good you look or feel in it. I think that is why Mila Kunis looks great in whatever she wears. If she doesn't feel good in it, she's not going to wear it.

Just so you know, the pressure never fades. I'm 50 years old and I still get pressure to buy things from other women. I was shopping recently with friends and I tried on pants that come to the ankle because that's what everyone is wearing these days. I have long legs and have always struggled to find pants that are long enough. Despite compliments from everyone around me, I couldn't feel comfortable in them. They looked good. But they didn't feel good to me. No matter how good of a deal they may have been or how many people told me they looked good, I know I wouldn't be comfortable in them, so I didn't buy them.

Consider Cost Per Wear

Clothing accounts for a large portion of a woman's spending, so it is important to get the most out of it. A technique my mother taught me to guide my wardrobe spending was to consider the cost per wear. If you buy a $10 t-shirt at a national discount chain and wear it once a month for the next two years, the cost per wear is $.42 (10.00 ÷ 24 = .42). If you buy a t-shirt at a designer boutique for $40 the cost per wear is $1.67 (40.00 ÷ 24 = 1.67).

When the average person is comfortable with the temperature in the room I am cold. As a result, blazers are a big part of my work wardrobe. When I find one I like and it fits well, I'm willing to spend $100-250 on it. The cost may be higher, but on average, I'll wear a blazer for seven to ten years. Depending on the weather and the fabric, I may wear it 12-24 times a year or 84 to 240 times. As a result, the cost per wear is somewhere between $0.63 and $1.79 per wear for a $150.00 jacket. That's about the same cost per wear as the t-shirt above.

I don't have a magic number for cost per wear because it depends on the clothing and my need. I may be willing to pay over a thousand dollars per wear for a wedding dress but less than $0.50 for a t-shirt.

Cost of Care

Mom also taught me the importance of taking care of my clothes so they would last, so the cost of care both in time and money have always been important factors for me. I periodically have to pay to dry clean my blazers, which I don't do for my t-shirts. I don't mind doing laundry or ironing when time allows, but I have concluded that a 100% cotton oxford is almost impossible to iron with satisfactory results, which means I try to buy wrinkle-free first. If I buy a 100% cotton blouse, I assume I'll be spending additional time and money having it dry cleaned after every wear.

Less Is More

Your shopping list should be based on what you NEED, not what is currently on sale. If it is an everyday item like toilet paper or milk, then take advantage of the sale. But if you don't need it now, stocking up on more t-shirts or Christmas decorations isn't going to add anything to your quality of life. It actually detracts from your quality of life by taking money you could be saving and adding more clutter in your home. The old adage is still very true: Less is more.

The less is more concept is the foundation of the tiny house trend. It is the realization that having more stuff doesn't add value to your life. My best friend has a small home on a big lake. Her and her family value being on a lake more than having more storage and stuff. If my friend buys a new dish or pillow, she has to get rid of an existing dish or pillow. It is a great and very intentional shopping strategy.

If You Aren't Sure, Walk Away

Big or small, if you aren't confident about a purchase, close your purse and walk-away. That unsure feeling is often your gut telling you something isn't right. Store clerks will reassure you and say you can always return it if you change your mind. They know once it leaves the store, it isn't likely to return. It is better not to buy it and go back if you change your mind than to buy it with the idea you might return it. The hassle factor alone limits what we will take the time to return, which is why so many products are promoted with a *money back guarantee*.

What's your budget?

Your budget is no one's business, particularly not a sales person's business. It is funny, but most sales people will find something to "fit your budget." If a sales person is asking you what you are looking to spend, they are either truly trying to narrow down what to show you so they don't waste your time or they are trying to get you to purchase the most expensive item. Trust your gut. You will be able to tell the difference.

This tactic is often used to justify large ticket items. The focus is put on the monthly payment instead of the total price. Anything can fit your monthly budget if you spread it over enough months.

You should always focus on the total cost. A lot of businesses make a TON of money from people who only look at the payment price and don't look at the total cost. Three payments of $19.95 sounds much better than $59.85. If it isn't something you are happy to pay $60.00 for today, you shouldn't pay $19.95 for it today, next month and the following month.

Marketers love "small" monthly payments because they know $20 a month sounds far better than $240 up front.

Avoid the Rush

Buy now! Only a few left! Don't miss out! While supplies last. These urgent calls to rush your decision are tactics to play to our human fear of being left out or not getting our share. It has nothing to do with the product. It has nothing to do with our need for the product, or the value of the product. But emphasizing a limited quantity or time to "get yours" forces us to rush to a decision, so we make a quick decision without thinking through whether or not we really need it.

Travel web sites and event ticketing use this trick extensively. While looking for a hotel room for a weekend away, pop-ups appear every 30 seconds, warning that, "Ten people booked this hotel in the last 24 hours." On event sites it is "Only 5 seats left in this section." And, "Twenty people searching for seats now." All these "Sale Ends Soon" tactics appeal to our desire to get what we want and make a purchase decision sooner than we would otherwise.

Starter Rates

Introductory offers, starter rates (like getting the first six months with 0% interest) and other initial rate offers are made to entice you to buy based on an initial rate that will only last a short time. These often come with long-term contracts that lock you into years of paying a significantly higher rate.

Read the fine print and evaluate these purchases based on the long-term price/rate that kicks in after the initial offer rate expires. If you would still make the purchase based on the long-term rate, then take advantage of the offer. If not, avoid the headache later and say no now.

Beware of Fine Print

The fine print can make a good deal go bad. The fine print on coupons, store shelf signs, and ads have made so many good deals go bad I rarely reference them for any buying decision. Too often I have grabbed something from the shelf that said "**$2.00 Off**" in big bold type, only to be told at the check-out counter that you have to purchase three bottles to get the $2.00 off. Of course, this is usually a product I only need to buy every three years, so the other two bottles I would purchase to "save" $2.00 would sit on my shelf at home for four years until they expire and I have to throw them out. Save yourself the frustration. If you need it and the regular price is reasonable, pull the trigger and make the purchase. If the regular price isn't reasonable, find it somewhere else.

Bulk Buying Only Works if You Need Bulk

Buying in bulk is rarely a deal unless you are buying for 20 people. Buying in bulk was a good savings strategy years ago, but that was before everything in America got SUPER-SIZED. You can no longer assume bigger will be better. More and more, I find the smaller container is a lower per unit price than the larger containers. Lately, I've found I can buy two smaller jars of an item for less than one large jar. I not only get more for my money, but it stays fresh longer with two separate jars.

Fees

Paying fees is how the poor stay poor. Payday loans, late fees, finance fees, service fees, convenience fees, administrative fees and the like disproportionately hit lower income Americans. There is a reason you generally find payday loan centers next to rental centers and high-risk insurance agents. They are all targeting lower income customers and living off the high fees they charge those customers.

Start looking at your bank statements, monthly bills, and purchase receipts to see what fees you regularly pay. If you don't know why you are paying a fee, ask. It can't hurt, and sometimes you find a fee can be waived or removed. Even if the fee can't be removed, you will at least know what you are paying and why.

Hit Delete!

Delete, Delete, Delete! Just like shopping in a big chain store, don't get sucked into online purchases because there is a "sale." The same rules apply to online shopping, but you have more control with your own inbox and online experience. Unless you've just made a purchase from the sender, I strongly recommend auto deleting all the vendor/retailer emails you receive.

Don't let retailers suck up your precious time by opening and reading their sales emails. The delete key can be you and your budget's best friend. Use it as a default for all retailer emails. If you discover later you need something from a particular retailer, you can always find it in your deleted items. You could also unsubscribe or use email system features that automatically file these emails when they hit your inbox. If you want to view them at some point they are available to you, but they aren't in your face every time you open your email.

Like in-store coupons, email sales and special offers almost always have quick expiration dates, exclusions, exceptions, and other crazy rules and requirements that make them worthless for many purchases. They are usually discounting what no one wanted to buy.

Crazy Claims

A repair shop manager once told me his shop's service was a better deal than the competition because, "We don't charge for labor," as if I was supposed to believe his employees worked for free. If someone is working on my car but not getting paid, I would either assume they were related to me and extremely nice or their knowledge and ability was so bad that they don't charge for it. Stay far away from the latter. When it comes to repairing something as important as a car, it's worth paying to have it done right!

Say No to Protection Plans

Service agreements and protection plans are rarely worth it. And in many cases, they make no sense at all. Recently, I purchased a low-end hand vacuum for $28. The clerk asked if I would be interested in the protection plan for $18, which would cover fixing the item or replacing it if it breaks. But if it breaks without a protection plan, for another $10 I can buy a brand new one with no paper work or hassle. Plus, I could choose to buy a newer model or a different brand.

My original cell phone protection plan was a reasonably price and covered a lot. As the years went by, what was covered was reduced and the cost increased. It got to the point where the cost wasn't worth the protection it provided. #Canceled.

Low Cost Retail Therapy

Retail therapy is a term that has become a popular way to describe a shopping binge to make you feel better. Had a bad day or a hard week? Go to the mall for a little "retail therapy."

It's true that getting out and walking around can be very therapeutic. Where some of us get into trouble, however, is when we are spending money to forget or avoid a problem. This form of retail therapy is like an addiction. What you use to avoid your problems and numb your feelings will compound the problem and add to the bad feelings. It only delays when you feel them.

Shopping isn't the same as spending. During most of my formative years, my parents were divorced and we had little money. Yet, my mom and I spent much of our free time shopping. We went to the mall, walked around and looked at all the latest fashions, critiquing as we went, stopping to evaluate only what really caught our eyes. We might get a pop or a small treat at the food court or meet one of my aunts for a bite to eat. It was a great night out without spending a lot of money.

The focus of these outings wasn't spending money on stuff; the focus was on getting out of the house, seeing what was new in the shops and popular culture, and occasionally splurging on a pop or ice cream and visiting with others. It is only now that I realize the side benefit of the exercise we got and the value of getting out of the house on cold Minnesota winter nights.

These outings were also the setting for some of our best conversations. We talked about what we liked and what we didn't like, what we would buy if we were rich, and what we wouldn't buy even if we were rich. These are great memories. I now think my mom may have taken me on these shopping trips partly because she enjoyed it, but also because it got me off the couch.

There was one store where we frequently window-shopped; it was a leather shop that also had jewelry. For months, we stopped in to see if the silver and black onyx bracelet Mom liked had dropped in price. One Mother's Day, my brother, sister and I pooled our money and bought her the bracelet. It was 35 years ago but I still remember the price. It was $30, which to us at the time was an enormous amount of money. It meant a lot to us to give her something we knew she wanted. Mom wore it throughout her life. When she passed away, it moved to my jewelry drawer. Whenever I wear it, I get complimented on it. I also get a special warm feeling.

The Latte Principle

The small stuff adds up! The latte principle basically means small regular expenses can quickly add-up. It was coined early in the Starbucks boom when folks started making expensive coffee part of their daily routine. At an average price of $3.65 for a latte, you could be spending $913 a year on coffee. That assumes one medium latte at $3.65 each day, five days a week for 50 weeks a year. That's also assuming two weeks when you don't buy one; if you bought one every day of the year, it would add up to $1,332. The key is being aware of what it costs you and being comfortable that it fits in your budget.

Just switching to a regular medium coffee at $1.70 would save almost $500 dollars a year. I confess I am a coffee gal! I would be happy eating chicken every night as long as I have my coffee every morning. And yes, I love mochas, but the cost and calories keep me from ordering it on a regular basis.

Simple Ways for doing the Math

What small changes in your spending habits could you make?

I strongly recommend adding the calculator feature to your smartphone's home screen so it is quick and easy to pull up. When looking at a price, round to the nearest whole amount. $14.99 becomes $15, and $47.99 becomes $50.

Do the rough math or take out your smartphone calculator to estimate the cost. If the sales rack says 25% OFF and the item you are considering is $50 (rounded), the mental math would look like this: 50% of 50 is 25. So half of 25 is 12.50. Your cost would be $50 - $12.50 = $37.50.

The smartphone calculation for the same item would look like this: 50.00 x 25%=12.50. So you'll "save" $12.50 when purchasing this $50 item. The resulting price will be around $37.50 ($50.00-$12.50=$37.50). Most calculators have a percentage key (%) in the expanded format. On my current phone, the expanded format appears when I turn my phone to view the screen horizontally. You can also convert the percent yourself by simply adding the decimal in front of the number, so 25% becomes .25. The resulting calculation is: 50.00 x .25 = 12.50. $50.00 - $12.50 = $37.50.

For 10%, move the decimal. So 10% of $34.99 is basically $3.50. You know this because you get $35.00 by rounding. Then, to see what 10% is you move the decimal one place to the left of the number and that tells you 10% of the original number, so 10% of 35.00 is 3.50. 10% of $50 is $5, and so on. The beauty of this simple calculation is any even percentage can then be multiplied by the ten percent amount. So 30% off of $50 is 3 times the 10% amount. In this case, $5.00 (10 percent of 50) X 3 = $15.00, so 60% off the same item would be 6 x $5.00 = $30.00.

Fine Print Game: Grab a pen and pick-up the Sunday paper. Grab the first insert ad you see. Set the timer on your smartphone to two minutes and hit start. Now circle as many fine print exceptions or misleading text as you can before the timer goes off. Here are the ones I found in the insert ad from a major national chain:

- Limited Quantities

- Save 35% off games. Select styles. Offers and coupons do not apply. * I was unable to find the * reference.

- Take an extra 20% off with this coupon. But half the items advertised have the note, "Offers and coupons do not apply. *" disclaimer.

- In very small print in the corner, "This product is not eligible for promotional offers and coupons. However, you are able to earn and redeem store bucks [also known as worthless funny money] and store reward points on this product. Visit our website or see associate for details."

- 40-50% Off All Outerwear for her. Excludes brand X.

How many did you find? Girl, your time and peace of mind are worth more than this insane paper chase! Plus, they are likely going to make you give personal information, like your email address, in order to redeem "reward points." In the meantime, you will receive a blur of endless emails with even more BIG Savings and small fine print.

We need to work just as hard to keep our money as others are working to get our money. It is your money. You worked hard for it. It is worth the extra effort to evaluate your purchases so you can keep as much of your money as possible.

As your financial footing gets stronger and your savings accounts grow, so will your financial confidence. You will question promotional claims about products and pricing, and you won't spend your money unless there is clear value for you. You will be a savvy shopper not easily swayed by "sales," ads, or a spokesperson. You will discover the joy of having enough for what is important to you. You will experience the freedom of making choices solely based on what is right for you. And in turn, you will set an example for others.

Chapter 10
Assets versus Liabilities

*God, grant me the serenity to accept
the things I cannot change,
the courage to change the things I can,
and the wisdom to know the difference.*

Serenity Prayer, author unknown

The Wisdom to Know the Difference

Understanding the difference between an asset and a liability is where most people get confused. An asset is something you own that has an economic value. Bank accounts, investments, and property you own are assets. If you still owe the bank or anyone else money related to it – it isn't yours yet.

To **own it**, it must be free of any obligation to anyone else. This is the beauty of ownership. It is yours, to do with it what you please, with no obligation to anyone. Just the sound of "no obligation" feels good, doesn't it?

Liabilities are financial obligations. Credit card debt, car loans, student loans, home mortgages and taxes are all liabilities. A common misconception people hold is that a car or a home is an asset. The truth is, they are only assets if you can afford the payments and obligations that come with them. As the Great Recession taught us, what looks like an asset can quickly turn into a liability if circumstances shift.

If you buy a house today with a $100,000 mortgage on it and tonight a wild fire burns it down, tomorrow you still owe $100,000 to the bank. That is why banks and mortgage companies require property insurance on homes they make loans on.

One of the most common financial mistakes made today is buying more car or house than you can afford. A car loses value the minute you drive it off the sales lot. This reduction in value is known as depreciation. The car continues to lose value every day you drive it. This has caused many to get behind financially. If you buy a new car for $30,000 with a loan for $27,000. Two years later it is worth $15,000 but you still owe $17,000. You owe $2,000 more than it is worth. If you wanted to sell it, it would actually cost you money. You would not only have to find a buyer at the current value of $15,000 but you would have to take all of the $15,000 you get from the sale, PLUS find another $2,000 to pay off the car loan.

A common term for this situation where you owe more than the value of the vehicle, property or stock option is called being "underwater." Too often people get underwater and panic. The panic adds to the problem. This may be how we got the term drowning in debt. There you are, playing in the water having fun and suddenly you are in over your head and at risk of drowning. Instead of calmly focusing on a solution panic sets in and you can't catch your breath or think clearly. You grab for anything that looks like a possible solution. But if you aren't careful what you grab for may just make it worse. Debt consolidation schemes, pay day loans and aggressive trade-in "deals" are a few examples of programs designed to take advantage of those in a tough situation. On the surface, they look like help but in reality and more often than not, they pull you into deeper water.

Assets can grow and make you rich. Liabilities, if not managed, can eat you alive financially and rob you of choices.

Let's take a closer look at a car purchase. Lilly and Ashley are twin sisters. They have different tastes and spending habits but the same amount of money. They both need a car so they are a good example of how purchase decisions can make a big impact on financial well-being.

Buying used vehicles is more economical and it is widely recommended. However, I am using new cars in this example to keep it simple, since mileage and condition are huge factors in vehicle value. The intent of the example is the same regardless if you are buying new or used. The key is to see the financial impact of large liability purchases.

Car Purchase			
	Lilly	Ashley	Difference
Out the Door Price	$31,057	$16,375	$14,682
Down Payment (20%)	$5,800	$3,056	$2,744
Amount Financed	$25,257	$13,319	$11,938
Loan Term	5 years	5 years	--
Monthly payment	$465	$245	$220
Total Paid Over 5 Years	$33,700	$17,756	$15,944

Figures from Kelly Blue Book (kbb.com).

Lilly likes the look and feel of the high-end models. Ashley likes those too, but would prefer to save more of her money. Having a lower car payment is more important to her than the comforts of additional features. The new car Lilly selected is $31,057. The new car Ashley selected is $16,375.

Both put twenty percent down and financed the remaining amount for five years at 4.00% annual percentage rate (APR). The difference between the two is the amount they paid for the car and the resulting additional interest. Lilly buys a car for almost double the price of the car Ashley buys. Because Ashley bought a less expensive model, she will save over $15,000. With expected trade-in value, that is more than enough to buy another brand-new car. In this case, Ashley could literally get two cars for the price of Lilly's one car.

With the savings on the purchase price and interest, Ashley will have an additional $220 a month to apply to other expenses or savings. That's $2,640 a year ($220 x 12 = $2,640).

At the end of five years, Lilly and Ashley both own their cars. That's when the cars really become assets—no strings or liabilities attached to them. After monthly payments for five years, the twins own their cars. At this point, they can keep driving them for the price of the operating costs (insurance, maintenance, and gas).

Even without a loan, vehicles are still depreciating assets. This means that the value continually goes down until they have no value, or worse, you have to pay to get rid of them. No matter how well you care for a vehicle, it loses value as time passes (excluding the very rare classic car), and it will eventually need to be replaced.

Like a car, a home can be an asset if you own it outright and you have available funds to pay for maintenance and upkeep. But the upkeep can suck you down if you don't have the money for it. A perfect example of this situation is my childhood home. It was the only home my parents purchased together. The first few years were great; it had lots of room and a big yard. My parents even bought the lot behind us so we'd have a bigger yard.

The situation changed dramatically when my parents separated. Dad stopped helping with the bills and what was a beautiful home quickly became a nightmare. Mom barely had money for the house mortgage, so the back lot went back to the original owner, along with the money my parents had already put into it. We went into debt every winter when the furnace needed oil. Every spring, the sump-pump broke down and the septic tank needed repair, and we went further into debt. Every day we lived there it cost us more than we could afford. What my parents thought was an asset became a huge liability.

There was some good news; Mom was able to sell the house, and it had appreciated enough in value that the sale price covered what Mom and Dad had put into it, plus the maintenance debts that had accumulated. Many who owned homes during the 2008 housing bust were not so lucky. They not only lost their homes to foreclosure, but also walked away with big debts, bankruptcy, and/or credit problems.

Luck can be a factor in financial well-being, but knowing the difference between an asset and a liability can keep you from getting in over your head.

Is a college education an asset or liability?

For too many, a college education has become a liability instead of an asset. Similar to how the 2008 Financial Crisis turned dream homes into a financial nightmare, student loan debt is turning the opportunity to get ahead into a liability that is weighing people down for the majority of their working life.

According to the National Center for Education Statistics, the average cost per year for a public college is $17,474 (2012/2013).[1] That's $70,000 for all four years. For private schools, it is double—$35,074 a year.

There are a lot of great colleges in this country, but you should do some serious career planning before spending $140,296 for a four-year degree ($35,074 x 4 = $140,296). Are the perks of a more expensive college worth an additional $70,000? It is a personal question, but one every girl who plans to go to college needs to ask herself.

College is like any purchase. You have to be honest with yourself about what you really need, how much it will cost, and the true value it will provide. Will paying more for the designer label be worth it long-term? Will the higher-cost option provide higher quality and outcomes, or does it just sound good? How much will it cost if four years stretch into five or six?

In a Martin Crutsinger article titled, *Most American Households Doing Better Financially*,[2] Crutsinger reported a couple important facts related to college degrees and financial well-being. Based on the Federal Reserve's annual survey on economic well-being, those with a college degree were more likely to report their financial situation had improved. Those with a high school degree or less were as likely to report a decline in their financial well-being as those reporting improvement in their financial well-being.

The same survey also showed almost half of those who attended a for-profit institution, in hindsight, would have attended a different school. That's a lot of people who regret their college choice!

With tens of thousands of dollars at stake, it is worth the time to do some fact finding. What are the job prospects for graduates with the degrees you're considering for your major? What is the average income for someone with that degree? Does the college where that degree was acquired make a difference? U.S. News & World Report EDUCATION website has some great resources to help with college research, debt and career prospects.[3]

The majority of jobs in America today require some education beyond high school, but this information has been used to fuel an accelerated competition among public and private colleges alike to attract students (and their dollars). With some families willing to pay whatever it takes to have their daughters attend the college of their choice, the demand for seats has increased. The colleges invest more to increase capacity—and raise tuition.

The American narrative has endorsed the idea that you must go to college, regardless of the cost. The belief is that you must have a degree to get a good job. As a result, huge amounts of money have been pouring into public and private colleges and entire industries have been created (and are profiting) from this craze.

The college prep industry alone has become massive. Students and their families are pouring money into ACT prep, college selection consultants, college ranking books and magazines, student activities to bolster high school "resumes," cross country college visit trips and more. Thousands of dollars are being spent on the selection process alone. This is before a person registers for a single class.

Colleges are spending millions on marketing to attract the attention of high school graduates. And the more competitive it gets, the more they spend to get the students.

Yes, jobs today and into the future require some post high school education. But, like any other large expense, you need to weigh the benefit against the cost. Is an eight-week commercial driver's license program that costs $4,500 more valuable than a four-year teaching degree? Based on the pay you are likely to receive, the commercial driver's license is more valuable in today's market. Of course, there are lifestyle and talent questions that are an important part of the equation, but if it is just about finance the commercial driver's license looks really good these days. Where I live, a licensed commercial driver can start with a salary around $41,000 a year, plus overtime. Those with experience and good records can make $65,000 plus with great benefits. And if they want, they can pursue a degree through online programs or weekend classes. Computer programmers, hardware technicians, and robotics technicians are all examples of good career tracks that don't require a four-year degree.

I am certainly not suggesting a four-year degree isn't of value. I have one and value the diploma and the doors it opened for me. I am suggesting you do the math and understand the alternatives to the traditional debt-funded degree programs in which most enroll, particularly when a four-year degree can take five plus years to get.

Let's look at another example with the twins. Assume they both love music. They played in the school band, sang in the choir and starred in the school musical. Both wanted to pursue music in college. Lilly pursued a degree in music performance. Ashley pursued a degree in music education. They attended the same college at the same cost; the only differences are the job prospects and the amount they were paid in their chosen careers after graduating.

Both twins got a good education. Both have four-year degrees. Both are employed. But Ashley has good career options, a strong salary and great benefits. She also helps with the school musical and sings with the local community choir.

Lilly is working at a local insurance company and sings with a band on weekends when they have a gig. She can barely make ends meet after making her student loan payments. Because she hasn't found many job prospects in music performance, she is also considering returning to school, which will require her to take out additional loans. With approximately a third of her income going to student loan payments, graduate school is out of the question right now.

According to student loan debt expert Mark Kantrowitz, if a person's annual income is more than their student debt total, they shouldn't have trouble paying the loans back in 10 years or less.[4] If the average salary for a graduate with the degree being considered is $140,000, then $140,000 of debt may be fine and reasonable. But if the average salary for the career being considered is only $70,000 or less, the student may have a problem paying off the debt.

Back to the question: Is a college degree or certificate an asset? The truth is, it depends. It depends on the debt associated with it *and* the earning potential it provides. A commercial driver's license certificate that costs $5,000 to get and allows the holder to get a job making $40,000 plus a year quickly becomes a valuable asset.

The value is really determined by what it allows you to do as a result of having it. A degree that required $200,000 in loans but only allows you to get a job earning $40,000 a year is more of a liability, unless the career path provides significant advancement opportunity.

These examples assume you complete the program and are able to get a better job as a result of having it. Where many get into trouble is taking on the debt but not completing the requirements to earn the degree or certificate. They end up with the liability but not the professional credentials to help pay for it.

Like many high-demand, high-cost purchases, the best deal often goes to the person who plays the game and negotiates the best deal. Being informed and willing to ask tough questions could save you tens of thousands of dollars.

Regardless of what others tell you, when taking on a large expense you need to ask yourself key questions. The first and most important question: Is this an asset or a liability? Other important questions include: Is it likely to increase in value or decrease in value? How long will it last? Is it worth the cost?

What if Lilly and Ashley asked these questions before taking out their student loans? What if Lilly and Ashley go to the same college for the same degrees but they work part-time during the school year and full-time on breaks and over the summer. Plus, they take advantage of online classes over the summer, and they're able to graduate in three years. With these strategies, they can graduate with $30,000 less in student loans. This provides the twins with the same asset (a degree) but a much smaller liability (debt). Plus, they have additional work experience, which will help them in future job searches and will provide them with valuable financial lessons and habits.

The more honest you are with yourself as you answer these questions, the happier you'll be with your decisions.

Chapter 11
Big Buys

He or she who is willing to be the most
uncomfortable is not only the bravest
but rises the fastest.

Brené Brown

Emotions Versus Logic: Act Your Wage!

Small splurges are good for the soul. They can be that reward you need to reinforce your positive habits. Splurging or over-spending on the big-ticket items is a much bigger deal. Splurging on a spa day or the "have to have" full leather designer boots that are THE Bomb may throw your plans off by weeks, months or years. With a few adjustments, you can make it work.

Home and auto purchases are where many of us get in over our heads. We want the big new home with amenities, the latest décor, and a tricked-out luxury car in the drive-way. It has become the picture of the American Dream—supersized! The problem is the live-for-today expenses hijack the security of our tomorrow. Over spending on a car or apartment can derail your long-term plans.

As we discussed earlier, it is important to know the difference between your personal worth and your net worth, but it is equally important to know the difference between your needs and your wants. Most of us need a car, but no one needs a hybrid hummer with surround sound and built-in bar for the seven days a year we tail-gate.

In much of American society, the type of car you drive is a symbol of your social status. According to the commercials on every channel, you aren't cool, worthy, intelligent, or good-looking if you aren't in a brand-new car.

If you combine the price of the average car with the emotional and social pressures of a vehicle purchase, the result is often gross overspending. Here are the common mistakes made with a vehicle purchase and how to avoid them. Note that I'm using an auto purchase as an examples, but many of the same mistakes are often made with other big purchases –appliances, furniture, boats, and houses, to name a few.

Mistake #1: Believing you are buying an asset instead of a liability. Too many purchase the nicest car they can based on the monthly payment they can squeeze into, instead of looking at the total price tag. As a result, they find out a year later they owe $25,000 on a vehicle that is only worth $20,000. Instead of having an asset worth $25,000, they have a liability of $5,000. This is a critical point worth repeating. The only time a vehicle is an asset is if you own it outright with no payments or obligations to anyone. And even if you do own it outright, the value of it will decrease with each passing month.

When you owe more than the value of the car, it is a hard situation to resolve. Even if you sell it, you still owe more than it is worth. To provide the buyer a clean title, you will have to pay the full amount of the loan you took out regardless of how much money you can get when you sell or trade it in.

Once you understand a vehicle will depreciate in value, you are better positioned to make a good decision. Even if you take good care of it, keep it clean and maintain it, it will lose value.

According to Edmunds.com, the average car depreciates 15-25% per year for the first five years.[1] It will continue to decrease with every mile driven. The only exceptions to this rule is if you are a mechanic or classic car investor who has the skills, knowledge, and tools to add value to the vehicle and WILL resell it.

If you buy a car today, know it will be worth less in six months and even less in two years. This means you have to treat it as a liability (expense) – not an asset. Don't get me wrong, I'm a car lover. There is something about driving a great car on a smooth open road that gives me joy. But I also enjoy the comfort of having money in the bank, so I have to weigh the two and find something that allows me a blend of comfort and joy.

Mistake #2: Making a purchase decision based on *emotion* instead of *need*. The *need* for a car is to get you safely to the places you need to go. *Emotions* tell us we should have a new car with all the bells and whistle and a brand that will make us look important and successful. What we actually *need* is a simple car that will get us to and from school or work for the next three years.

Mistake #3: Not factoring in cost of ownership. Cost of ownership includes things like price of insurance, gas consumption (measured by miles per gallon), and average maintenance costs.

I once test drove a cool SUV that was on "sale" at a local dealer. It was a great vehicle; I felt like a queen as I sat up high and drove it around town. Back at home, I pulled out the calculator to figure out the cost difference in miles per gallon as compared to the other less royal vehicle I was planning to buy. Based on the average number of miles I normally drive and the number of years I was planning to keep the vehicle, I determined the SUV would cost an additional $6,000 over the life of the car in gas alone. Since I had small children at the time and was saving for their college education, the $6,000 represented a semester's worth of college for one of my kids (note gas prices were higher then). While I loved the royal feeling I had when driving the bigger SUV, I quickly decided it was better to fund a child's education than to spend the same amount on gas with nothing to show for it.

Using the same cars in the purchase example in Chapter 10, the five-year cost of ownership for Ashley's car is $28,666 as compared to Lilly's five-year cost of ownership at $40,502. Interestingly, the majority of the approximately $12,000 difference between the two cars is depreciation ($8,932) and fuel costs ($1,253).

Mistake #4: Leasing instead of buying a car. When it comes to personal finances, it is better to buy a car than to lease a car. Leases are car rental arrangements where you make a down payment plus monthly payments for a couple of years and at the end of the lease you own <u>nothing</u>! On top of that, you could owe even more if you go over the mileage limit or get hit with wear and tear charges. You are better off taking the same amount of money you would have used for the lease and use it to purchase a car.

Here's an example of a lease on a popular luxury car. The three-year arrangement would cost almost $20,000, assuming no mileage or wear and tear fees. If you are going to spend $20,000 on a car, shouldn't it be on one you can keep or sell as you please instead of giving it back and having nothing to show for it?

Based on the ad, the lease requires monthly payments of $419 for 36 months (419 x 36 = 15,084), plus $3,999 as a down payment. The result is $19,083. You could buy a nice car for $19,083, and you could put on as many miles as you like without having to pay extra for every mile over 10,000 each year.

According to an August 14, 2016 ad in my area paper, a small economy car lease will cost you $7,563 for three years, plus maintenance, wear and tear fees, and $.15 for any miles over the 12,000 per year limit. It is much less than the luxury car, but you still have nothing in the end.

One of the reasons leases have become popular is because it is used as a way to drive "more car" than you can otherwise afford. While many consider this an advantage, to me it is the biggest reason not to do it.

When you sign a lease, you are in it for the duration; when you purchase you have more options. You can trade it in or sell it if your needs change. There are some cases that might justify a lease, but those cases are rare so I will leave car leases on the list of things not to do.

Mistake #5: Buying on impulse. This is associated with buying based on emotion and failing to do your research. Car dealers know many car purchases are based on emotion, so they fill their lots with the high-end, fully-loaded car styles. When you test-drive a car, they sit you in a plush model, with all the bells and whistles. Of course, you will love it. It has everything you need and $5,000 to $10,000 of things you don't need. Instead of focusing on the basics, they point out the adjustable leather seats, the seven-speaker audio system, and the fancy technology and navigation system. That's because a lot of the profit in a vehicle comes from these expensive add-ons.

When you decide the car is for you in this situation, you are deciding based on the add-ons. Of course, the dealer has plenty in stock in every color you could want. But if you ask for the base model, without the leather seats, seven-speaker audio, and navigation system, you often have to wait weeks... or they only have one available and it is in an unpopular color. As a result, they talk you into a car with $4,000 of features that aren't essential to your needs and will only add a couple hundred dollars to the resale value.

Mistake #6: Not researching what you are buying. What looks great on the sales lot is often the car that isn't going to last more than a few miles down the road. This good-looking car is like the frat boy player on campus. It might look and sound great on Friday night, but it's a nightmare the following week and adds months of regret to your life.

Fortunately, you don't need to be a mechanic to research a car these days; there are plenty of resources available. Kelly's Blue Book (kbb.com) has a wealth of information on every make and model.[2] Plus, they have consumer reviews, average prices paid for similar cars, and estimates of lifetime cost of ownership.

Edmunds.com is another good online car buying resource.[3] It's also worth every penny to get Consumer Reports Buying Guide. Buying a car is expensive, and knowing as much as possible before you purchase it is worth the time. Once you've signed the paperwork, assume it is yours until you sell it or trade it. Don't rely on state lemon laws to protect you.

I'm a fan of Consumer Reports Auto Ratings.[4] They do extensive research and provide overall ratings on almost all cars by class, making it easy to compare across styles and makes. It also provides a history on major maintenance issues. It is important to maintain a car well but I *hate* bringing my car to the shop, so I'll pay more to do it less often. Consumer Reports has more than once shown me that the cars with high maintenance problems are sometimes also the higher priced cars. It has saved me from making a double mistake. I recommend getting this in hard copy form versus their online version because it is easier to compare across models and reference when car shopping. I realize you might think that is old school, but the paperback version can also be cheaper than buying multiple online reports for the different models you are considering.

Research is great, but don't forget to take time to test-drive the vehicles you are researching. Nothing can replace what you learn when you climb in behind the wheel and take it for a spin. You'll discover the amount of legroom you really need, or where you'll put your bag.

A hands-on test once saved me thousands of dollars. I had done all my research on the car I wanted. My husband and I had driven it and decided on the more expensive model that had a third-row seat. Before we ordered it, I stopped by the dealership to look at color options.

My seven-year-old son was with me. While showing him the car we planned to purchase, I let him climb into the third-row seat. In the process, I discovered the third row, which is why we were buying the bigger model, was hard for him to get in and out of and had little legroom, even for a seven-year-old. We have two kids, so the third row was a luxury for when our children brought more than one friend. As a result of that discovery, we opted for a less expensive model with more cargo space but no third row. Now it is my son's car. He is in college and appreciates the extra cargo space for all his gear, and it has room for three friends comfortably.

Buying a Home

Buying a home is like a car purchase on steroids. Emotions run high and the wish list of features is long! With the average existing home price in the U.S. at $244,100, it is worth doing your homework. If you decide purchasing a home is right for you, here are a few tips.

1. **Re-read mistake number three!** A home is one of the most emotional purchases you can make. It is also where you are most likely to fall in love with a particular area or property and lose sight of financial facts. Picking a house based on emotion is like picking a spouse solely on physical looks. The wedding photos may be nice, but the marriage could be long and painful.

   The process of house hunting can be emotionally draining, as well. Your judgment can easily get clouded if you aren't careful. Women are wired for nesting. As a result, when we compare homes, we aren't just comparing features, prices, and locations; we are comparing how each home makes us feel. We consider what our friends will think and if there is room for our parents to stay when they visit. There is a lot more to it then price and number of bathrooms.

2. **Don't buy unless you plan to stay at least five years.** The first few years in a home are generally the most expensive. In addition to the price of the home, there are upfront closing costs associated with a home purchase. According to Zillow.com, closing costs on a $150,000

home may be between $3,000 and $7,500.[5] These costs are real but add no value to the property.

The first few years of mortgage payments go largely to pay interest. Unless you are in a rapidly appreciating area, little equity accumulates in the early years. These early years also have expenses for updates, furniture, window coverings and other décor, which may not add to the value of the home.

3. **Set your price range based on your budget.** Do NOT set your price range based on what a mortgage company will loan you! What a lender says you can "afford" and what is right for you and your goals are two different amounts. As we saw during the financial crisis (aka the Great Recession), mortgage companies are usually willing to loan you more than you want to spend. A mortgage broker's goal is to make money by making loans. The bigger the loan the bigger the sales commissions. Your goal is to not be house poor.

    House poor is a term used when someone has purchased more home then they can comfortably afford. As a result, they don't have money to purchase furniture, make upgrades, or do anything other than work in order to make the house payments.

    Remember, with bigger homes come bigger utility bills and bigger neighborhood expectations. I believe the less you need to be comfortable when you are young, the more financially comfortable you will be when you are old.

4. **It isn't an asset unless it is worth significantly more than you owe on it *and* you can comfortably manage the costs of ownership (mortgage, utilities, maintenance, lawn care, etc.).** Many learned this the hard way during the Great Recession. With a bad market and a couple missed payments, you can go from home owner to homeless and bankrupt.

5. **Include cost of ownership in your purchase decision.** Even if you were lucky enough to pay cash for your

home there are always costs to ownership, which includes property taxes, utilities, repairs, insurance and general upkeep. The more you research and plan for these costs, the better you can handle the surprise repairs, unexpected spikes in heating or cooling costs, or increases in property taxes.

6. **Shop as much for your mortgage as you do your home.** Rates and terms vary greatly from lender to lender, so call and ask what terms they will offer you. Doing so can save you thousands of dollars.

   If done within a concentrated period of time, rate shopping is factored in your credit score; this means it will have little impact on your score over the long-term. If you are concerned with the inquiries into your credit, get a copy of your current credit report and score. Share as appropriate with lenders to get a specific rate quote for the price range you are considering.

7. **Get pre-approved for a mortgage.** Once you've found the mortgage provider you like (the one that will provide the best terms and rate), get pre-approved. In a competitive housing market this can give you an edge over other buyers. It also helps you know what your rate, terms, and payments will be. Note, until you lock in a rate, mortgage terms are subject to change.

8. **We are in an era of low interest rates.** Take advantage of them and get a fixed rate mortgage. If you can stretch yourself to make a 15 or 20-year mortgage payment, it is worth doing. If not, get a 30-year fixed rate mortgage and plan to make additional payments. Just adding $50 to your payment each month can reduce your loan term by a few years and save you significant money on the average loan.

9. **Learn the number one rule in real estate: Location, location, location.** What's the school district like? Is crime an issue? Do your homework and learn as much about the area as you can. Spend time there. Are there

major changes expected in the area? Is the area growing, shrinking or remaining the same?

10. **Focus on the things you can't easily change.** Location and lot size are the most obvious things you can't change. Unless you budget for the high cost of adding square footage or modifying the structural layout, it is what it is. No paint color or flooring covering will change it.

11. **Trust but verify.** If your purchasing decision is based on something you are told by someone who benefits from you making the purchase (like a real estate agent), it is worth verifying. If you are buying because the empty lot next door will be a park, call the city and ask for confirmation that it will be a park and not a parking lot.

12. **If you find the right home for you, make your offer contingent on an independent inspection.** A proper home inspection will check the structural, electrical, plumbing, and other major components of a home—like the roof, siding, plumbing and furnace. These are the typical problem areas and are pricey to repair/replace. A home inspection will not find all defects, but it should point out major repairs or issues. An inspection helps avoid buying a money pit and helps you better understand what you are buying. If at all possible, be at the inspection. You will see the property in a new light when the focus is on the fundamentals instead of how nice your furniture will look in the living room. Furniture is easy to change. The roof is not.

13. **Put down twenty percent.** Putting 20% down not only reduces the amount you are borrowing, but it is the amount needed by most lenders to avoid paying for private mortgage insurance (PMI). PMI protects the lender should you default on your loan. Rates vary based on loan amount, credit score, and company. Monthly PMI charges commonly cost $50 to $150 per month, so you want to avoid it or get rid of it as soon as possible. This money is much better spent on your loan principal.

14. **If you currently own a home and are buying a new home, make the purchase of the new home contingent on the sale of your current home.** If you don't, you could easily end up with two house payments, two utility bills and one big headache. The equity or appreciation you have in your existing home could be lost to carrying costs associated with a house you no longer live in.

Big buys can come with big rewards or big regrets. Buying an impractical outfit may not be a great financial buy, but in a year or two it won't matter and you won't remember it. An impulsive car purchase can stick with you for years. A poor choice in a home purchase can cause you headaches for decades.

I emphasize the long-lasting nature of these big buys not to scare you out of the decision, but to motivate you to invest the time and effort to understanding exactly what you need. Understand what you are getting and what it will cost you. Understand your options and be comfortable with the associated financial consequences. You can't return a home or a car for store credit or rely on a money back guarantee. A little upfront research will pay off big on these purchases.

Chapter 12
Dealing with Debt

*Be under obligation to no one – the only obligation
you have is to love another.*

Romans 13:8

Debt should be AMP'ed

I have three basic rules for dealing with debt: AMP

1. **A**void it
2. **M**inimize it
3. **P**lan for it

Rule #1: Avoid debt as much as possible. There are no secrets or magic here, just old school common sense. Save for what you need and want and pay for it once you have enough saved to buy it. This is the back to the basics—farm to table—type recipe for financial health. It's not sexy or fancy, but it may seem exotic since so few do it.

Rule #2: If you can't avoid it, minimize it. Car, home, or student loans are good examples of purchases that may justify going into debt.

When you save up and pay cash, the purchase is one big price tag. But when you borrow the money for the same purchase, it gets convoluted by additional interest and fees, and then broken into monthly payments. Somehow $199 per month sounds so much better than $11,940.

It often takes less time to get a bachelor's degree than it does to pay off a used car loan. Focusing on the total price instead of the monthly payment helps reduce temptations to take on more debt. Every $1 you spend in cash is likely equal to spending $1.05 to $1.70 in debt. The more you minimize the debt, the better off you'll be.

Rule #3: Have a plan for loan payment BEFORE you take it out. It is easy to get focused on the impressive degree or shiny car when you are borrowing money. Hyper focus on what you get can distract you from the reality of what you will have to give in return. There are two sides to every transaction. If you aren't clear on how you will make the payments and how long you'll have to make them, you aren't ready to take out the loan.

The "wait and save" time period may be frustrating, but it often has side benefits. During the wait, new information may come to light that impacts your purchase decision. Waiting to buy the next technology upgrade usually results in the availability of a newly released model. Waiting a few months has forced me to find alternative solutions with what I already own. Multiple times I've found I had something I could make work, or that what I really needed was something different than what I was planning to buy.

Debt Payment Strategies

You need to protect your credit by maintaining all loans in good standing. Maintaining good standing means you are up-to-date with all expected payments. Lenders receive your regular payments on time and as expected.

If you ever have a problem with your loan or payment, contact the lender and communicate with them openly and honestly about the situation and work with them to resolve any issues. Be polite and upfront. Ask questions if there is anything you don't understand. If you were late with one payment it is fair to ask if they can waive the late fee. It is okay if they say no. Be respectful. They don't owe you, you owe them.

My favorite high school teacher taught me this important lesson in navigating high school in good standing. He told me to follow my teacher's rules, be polite, and show respect. He told me if I follow the rules of those in authority 90% of the time, they would likely cut me some slack the 10% of the time when I needed it. Dealing with creditors can be the same. If you follow their rules the majority of the time, they are more likely to cut you some slack the one month your payment hits the day after it was due.

If any of your accounts aren't in good standing, call the lender(s) and ask them what it will take to get the account back into good standing. Like high school teachers, most lenders will work with you if you communicate with them and do your part. The sooner you make the call, the easier it will be. Your phone is likely within reach right now so make the call. Even if you aren't sure what to say, just call. Lenders have staff to help you.

Once all your debt accounts are in good standing, it is time to start playing whack-a-debt. It is like the carnival game whack-a-mole, where you pay $2.00 to smack moles that pop out of holes. Whack-a-debt has all of the moles outside of their holes and you need to smack them down payment by payment to make them go away. Some will require more whacks than others. That's okay. Just keep whacking.

Payoff Strategies

There are a number of strategies for paying off debt. Those who focus on behavioral adjustments suggest paying off the smallest loan first; enjoy a nice mental victory and then start on the next one (second smallest). These mental wins are very motivating. They come with the added bonus of simplifying the bill paying process and reduced hassle factor of having one less loan.

Math geeks, of course, look at the pure finance side and say you should pay off the loans with the highest interest rate first. This too is solid advice, particularly, if one has a significantly higher rate than the other(s).

Others suggest you pay off by class or type of debt. This would include all credit cards, all store or retail debt including home improvement, appliances/furniture or anything that is not a student, car, or home loan. Once the credit card and retail debt is paid, then tackle the car and student loan, leaving the home loan for last. By nature of the loans offered in the different classes, it often mirrors paying off the highest interest rate loan first.

Another consideration is the duration of the loan. If your car loan is due to be paid off in 12 months, you could work to pay it off sooner. Then, add the amount of the car payment you had been making to your monthly student loan payment. The bottom line of your budget stays the same, but you can significantly reduce the duration of your student loan.

I recommend you get rid of the small, expensive debt first. This would include credit card balances of any kind. Once those are gone, work to pay off any other personal loans, like a loan for furniture or appliances. Next up, tackle any student and/or auto loans. Which one you should focus on first depends on many factors like interest rate, duration of the loan, size of the loan, etc. Your motivation also plays a role. If the loans are similar in size and rate, then go after the one you are most motivated to pay off. Motivation can be more powerful than the numbers, so factor it into your plan and use it to your advantage. With all of these strategies, a home loan would usually be the last loan to pay off.

Should I postpone retirement savings to pay-off debt?

It is common to ask the question, **"Should I put off saving for retirement while I'm paying off my student (or other) loans?"** My answer is NO.

First, the question pits two great practices against each other, as if it is impossible to do both. If it truly is impossible to do both, you have to pay your obligations first, obviously. But a better question would be, "Can I reduce my spending in other ways so I can pay my obligations AND pay myself (save for retirement)?" If you ask yourself this question you will find ways to put some money into your retirement savings. Even if it is only a few dollars to start, it is worth doing! As with anything, the first step is the hardest. As you see even small amounts grow, you will find ways to add more as your debts go down.

Second, not saving for retirement forfeits the advantage of time. You can't get it back, and you are fooling yourself if you think saving more later will make up for it. Feel free to look ahead to the Magic of Starting Early illustration in Chapter 14: The Magic of Saving and Investing.

Third, it breaks the rule of paying yourself first. It doesn't support establishing a strong savings habit, and by putting debt first it actually rewards your spending habit.

And, finally, postponing one for the other is just another form of procrastination. Put on your big girl pants and find a way to save a little and pay off your debts at the same time.

Debt is like a pile of smelly garbage in your home. It is often necessary but you want to get rid of it as soon as possible. All of these strategies work because they are focused on the same goal: paying off debt. No matter how you do it, you can't go wrong paying off debt.

Chapter 13
Insure for a Good Night's Sleep

Fun is like life insurance;
the older you get, the more it costs.

Kin Hubbard

Insure for Unpredictable Loss

Insurance gets a bad reputation; it is dull and has a lot of fine print. Think of it this way: Insurance is like a spare tire. It is important to have but you hope you never have to use it.

At its core, insurance is designed to take small regular payments from a large group of people so funds are there to help the few impacted by tragedy (events like tornadoes, a horrific car accident or cancer). These are hard to predict and only the rich could save enough to cover the financial consequences they can cause.

This chapter is a high-level overview of the key insurance coverage a young person should have. It is not a comprehensive review of all insurance types or options. Insurance varies by state, so talk to a local agent or broker. Get multiple quotes to find the best deal for your needs.

What Insurance Do You Need?

Medical/Health

Everyone needs medical insurance – regardless of your age or risk. You never know when an accident or medical condition will hit. If it does, you want to be covered; even a relatively small accident or illness could cost tens of thousands of dollars.

Medical insurance these days often includes wellness benefits like free annual exams, recommended screenings, and discount fitness club memberships. Take advantage of them. Your health is one of the best investments you can make. It will pay off in good health and lower costs throughout your life.

The cost of medical care and the insurance associated with it has been increasing for years (both before and after the implementation of the Affordable Care Act). If you are 26 years old or younger, you can be covered under your parent's plan. This is a great deal! Take advantage of it if you can.

The next best deal is often getting it through an employer, which may be a better deal than coverage with your parent's insurance. If that's not an option, go to an insurance broker or a government exchange like HealthCare.gov.[1] If the Trump administration changes the Affordable Care Act, this government web site should provide information on replacement options.

If you are not able to purchase insurance through an employer, I recommend buying from a large established carrier who has been in the medical insurance business for a number of years. You want a carrier who will be around when you need them. You also want to make sure the network of doctors accessible with the specific insurance plan is acceptable to you (i.e., you can see the doctor you want).

Car Insurance

If you have a car, you need auto insurance. Let me be really clear. If you have a motorized vehicle that you intend to drive on public roads, you need insurance for it.

All states except New Hampshire and Virginia require drivers to have at least liability insurance.[2] In New Hampshire, you don't have to have insurance if you can demonstrate you can pay damages in case of an accident. Since damages can easily go into the millions, leave it to the pros and buy insurance! If you are going to tempt fate, do it with something more fun than insurance.

Liability coverage is the bare minimum you should have on any vehicle no matter how much it is worth. It will not pay for damage to your vehicle, but it does cover damage you may cause to someone else (personal injury) or their property (property damage).

Collision and comprehensive coverage pays for damage to your vehicle and property. This coverage is not required by law. Collision provides coverage if you are in an accident, while Comprehensive covers damage caused by things like hail, tornadoes, theft, and the inevitable windshield rock chip.

There are many factors in the price of auto insurance you can't control, so focus on those you can: your credit score, your car, the coverage you select, including deductibles, and your driving record. There are always some state exceptions, but in general, the better your credit score the lower your premium. The more sporty or expensive your car, the more your insurance will cost. And, the more speeding tickets or driving violations and accidents you have on your record, the more you'll pay for car insurance.

If you have some savings and can afford to cover the first $500 to a $1,000 if you are in an accident or hail storm, buy a policy with a $500 or $1,000 deductible. The higher your deductible, the lower your premium. A higher deductible can save you hundreds of dollars a year. If you go without having an accident or claim for three to five years, you'll have saved enough to cover the deductible if something does happen. Of course, that assumes you put the money you saved in the bank and didn't spend it online on Cyber Monday.

Your need for Collision and/or Comprehensive coverage is largely determined by how much your vehicle is worth and how much the coverage costs. If your car is worth $2,500, having collision and/or comprehensive coverage has a lot less value than if your car is worth $15,000, particularly if you have a $500 or $1,000 deductible. Your risk tolerance and savings are big factors when considering these types of coverage.

If you have a loan on the vehicle, the financing company will require Collision and Comprehensive insurance. This protects the property (collateral) of the loan. It ensures the bank will get their money back if the car is damaged due to a collision or a storm.

Renter's Insurance

Renter's insurance covers all of your stuff. If you are renting where you live, the property will be covered by your landlord's insurance but it will not cover the stuff you own. Your furniture, computers, clothing, and collections aren't covered unless you have a renter's insurance policy. Renter's policies also include liability coverage, which is always good to have.

Renter's policies are generally inexpensive. They are usually less than $20 a month. So if you have a lot of valuable stuff, it is worth getting a policy.

Homeowner's Insurance

The rule here is easy. If you own a home (house, condo, townhome, etc.), you need homeowner's insurance; it will be required if you have a loan. The basic terms and options of these policies are very similar, so do what you can to minimize your costs.

Key factors in the cost of your policy include your credit score or credit rating (insurance rating in states that don't allow credit scores to be used), claims history, deductible, and options you select.

Like car insurance, get the highest deductible you can comfortably afford. If you can go a couple years without a claim, you can often save enough to cover the deductible portion of a loss or accident you may have. Not long ago I increased the deductible on our homeowner's policy. As a result, we are now saving about $300 a year on our premium. In a few years, we'll have saved enough to cover the higher deductible should we have a claim.

Disability Insurance

Disability income insurance replaces a portion of your income if you become too sick or injured to work. Since your ability to earn an income is one of your biggest assets, it is worth insuring.

The two primary types of disability insurance are short-term and long-term. As the labels suggest, the primary difference between them is the length of coverage. Short-term disability policies are designed to provide some income replacement for a short period of time. If you fall and break a leg over the weekend and can't work for a few months, short-term disability (STD) insurance can help you pay the bills for a short period of time. STD policies generally provide benefits for three to six months, depending on the policy and the benefit period. A good emergency savings account can provide the same safety net but requires strong discipline. Without the self-discipline to create and keep three to six months' worth of expenses set aside, you are at risk of having a common bad break become the thing that caused you to go broke.

Long-term disabilities are the most financially devastating. It would be difficult if you couldn't make a living for a few months, yet most could financially recover. However, if you can't earn an income for two years, or maybe even the rest of your life, your standard of living will dramatically change and you may never recover. This is where long-term disability (LTD) insurance comes in.

Through family members, I have personally seen the significant impact having and not having LTD has on a person's quality of life. That is why I recommend having LTD coverage to everyone who relies on their ability to earn an income to maintain their lifestyle. I've had my policy since my late 20s. It's not a fun check to write, but I sleep better knowing I have it.

The three key components of disability coverage arc the elimination period (how long you wait before benefits start to pay), the benefit period (how long benefits last), and the definition of disability (determines when benefits pay). A longer elimination period is like having a higher deductible. The longer it is, the less the coverage costs. When looking at disability coverage, ask for quotes for multiple elimination periods to see what waiting an extra month or two for benefits might save you in annual premiums.

Don't skimp on the benefit period. If available, get coverage to age 65. There is a reason it is called long-term disability. If you need it, you want it to last as long as possible.

The definition of disability is also very important. This is particularly true if you are in a highly compensated or specialized field—engineer, doctor, lawyer, etc.

For example, say you are an engineer who is a few years into your career, making $85,000 per year. You are in a car accident with head injuries. You can no longer perform the difficult calculations and thought processes of an engineer. If you have a policy that defines disability as your inability to perform *any* occupation, it means if you can perform the duties of *any* job you may not be eligible for benefits. As a result, you will not only have to adjust to your disability, but to an income a small fraction of what it was.

Life Insurance

If someone is financially dependent on you, then you should have life insurance. Being a parent is the most obvious situation, but it could be a spouse, aging parent, or anyone you want to make sure would have financial resources if you weren't around to help provide for them.

Keep it simple. Buy term life insurance. If you are young and healthy, it is going to be inexpensive and easy to get. The older you are when you purchase it the more it will cost, so there is an advantage to buying it when you are young.

Term life insurance only lasts for the stated <u>term</u>. Typical term options are 10, 20 or 30 years. It provides the stated death benefit to the person(s) you designate as a beneficiary if you die during the stated term. What I like about term life insurance is it is simple, straight-forward and inexpensive.

One other option to consider when buying term insurance is if it has a conversion feature. Some term insurance can be converted to permanent insurance without proof of insurability (meaning regardless of your current health). I had a friend that had term insurance with such a conversion feature who got cancer. She was nearing the end of her term for insurance coverage—meaning her 20-year term was expiring. She was able to convert her term insurance to permanent insurance to ensure the coverage would continue for her life, and her dependents would receive those funds.

For all of the insurance types discussed above—especially home, auto and life—be sure to shop around. Be sure you trust and like your insurance agent and company, as you will likely talk with them more than once during your lifetime. Also, be sure to re-shop and re-price your coverage every 3-5 years to ensure the price that you are paying is competitive and you are getting a good value.

Section 3
Make Your Money Grow

Formal education will make you a living;
self-education will make you a fortune.

Jim Rohn

You'll know you have a true asset when it starts making money for you. That is the ultimate goal of personal finance: To have your money work for you. Having enough to cover your expenses and have a comfortable lifestyle is great, but having a lifestyle supported by the money your money is making is even better.

Chapter 14
The Magic of Saving and Investing

Compound interest is the eighth wonder of the world.
He who understands it, earns it ...
he who doesn't ... pays it.

Albert Einstein

How the Rich Get Richer

The old saying, *the rich get richer* isn't a myth or an old wives tale. It is a saying based on the fact that those who have money and invest it wisely usually grow their wealth and become wealthier as a result. So, the rich often do get richer. Not only is it totally appropriate, but if they didn't our economy would suffer. Their investments provide jobs and loans for others. It is no secret. You can do it too!

Making a lot of money doesn't grow your wealth. Growing wealth is about how much you keep—not how much you earn. Nicolas Cage, Kanye West, and a long list of other famous high-income earners learned this lesson when they had financial trouble because their expensive lifestyle exceeded their high income. If you spend more than you earn, you will still be broke. No matter how many records you have sold or movies you are in, the math is the same. *If you spend more than you earn, you go broke.*

The rich save and let their money work for them. Instead of paying someone else interest, they have others paying them interest. Over time it builds on itself until the money becomes a source of income.

Let's look at the twins again. Lilly and Ashley have very different careers, but both make $45,000 a year and live in the same metro area.

Lilly loves living in the trendy part of town. As we saw in Chapter 10: Assets v Liabilities, Lilly also likes more expensive cars. This doesn't leave her much for savings. Her twin sister, Ashley, rents an apartment in a suburb and drives a lower-end car. This allows her to invest $167 per month, giving her $2,000 a year to invest in a mutual fund.

Lilly knows she should be saving but she hasn't found the job that really fits her yet. Plus, her shopping habit takes up most of her time and money. She tells herself that once she's in a job she likes, she will start saving.

The twins' cousin, Maddy, is the same age as Lilly and Ashley. Maddy is in sales. Her income fluctuates but is consistently higher than both Lilly's and Ashley's. Maddy uses her high income on luxury items and high-end fashion. As a result, she spends more than her income and goes into debt. Since she has a high income, she figures she'll catch up on her savings by saving more later. She plans to save twice as much when she is in her forties.

Starting at age 25, Ashley saves $2,000 a year for 20 years. Lilly starts at age 35 and saves $3,000 a year for 20 years. Maddy starts saving at 45. To make up for lost time, Maddy saves $4,000 for 20 years. We will assume all three earn a 5% return on their savings. The only difference is the amount saved and the age at which they started to save.

Logic might tell you the one who saves the most will have the biggest account balance. Surely, if Maddy saved twice as much money as Ashley, she'd have a correspondingly higher amount of money in the end. But when time and compound interest are part of the equation, small amounts can win big.

The Magic of Starting Early

Age	Ashley Investment	Ashley Balance	Lilly Investment	Lilly Balance	Maddy Investment	Maddy Balance
25	$	$ 0	$ 0	$ 0	$ 0	$ 0
26	$ 2,000	$ 2,100	$ 0	$ 0	$ 0	$ 0
27	$ 2,000	$ 4,305	$ 0	$ 0	$ 0	$ 0
28	$ 2,000	$ 6,620	$ 0	$ 0	$ 0	$ 0
29	$ 2,000	$ 9,051	$ 0	$ 0	$ 0	$ 0
30	$ 2,000	$ 11,604	$ 0	$ 0	$ 0	$ 0
31	$ 2,000	$ 14,284	$ 0	$ 0	$ 0	$ 0
32	$ 2,000	$ 17,098	$ 0	$ 0	$ 0	$ 0
33	$ 2,000	$ 20,053	$ 0	$ 0	$ 0	$ 0
34	$ 2,000	$ 23,156	$ 0	$ 0	$ 0	$ 0
35	$ 2,000	$ 26,414	$ 0	$ 0	$ 0	$ 0
36	$ 2,000	$ 29,834	$ 3,000	$ 3,150	$ 0	$ 0
37	$ 2,000	$ 33,426	$ 3,000	$ 6,458	$ 0	$ 0
38	$ 2,000	$ 37,197	$ 3,000	$ 9,930	$ 0	$ 0
39	$ 2,000	$ 41,157	$ 3,000	$ 13,577	$ 0	$ 0
40	$ 2,000	$ 45,315	$ 3,000	$ 17,406	$ 0	$ 0
41	$ 2,000	$ 49,681	$ 3,000	$ 21,426	$ 0	$ 0
42	$ 2,000	$ 54,265	$ 3,000	$ 25,647	$ 0	$ 0
43	$ 2,000	$ 59,078	$ 3,000	$ 30,080	$ 0	$ 0
44	$ 2,000	$ 64,132	$ 3,000	$ 34,734	$ 0	$ 0
45	$ 2,000	$ 69,439	$ 3,000	$ 39,620	$ 0	$ 0
46	$ 0	$ 72,910	$ 3,000	$ 44,751	$ 4,000	$ 4,200
47	$ 0	$ 76,556	$ 3,000	$ 50,139	$ 4,000	$ 8,610
48	$ 0	$ 80,384	$ 3,000	$ 55,796	$ 4,000	$ 13,241
49	$ 0	$ 84,403	$ 3,000	$ 61,736	$ 4,000	$ 18,103
50	$ 0	$ 88,623	$ 3,000	$ 67,972	$ 4,000	$ 23,208
51	$ 0	$ 93,054	$ 3,000	$ 74,521	$ 4,000	$ 28,568
52	$ 0	$ 97,707	$ 3,000	$ 81,397	$ 4,000	$ 34,196
53	$ 0	$ 102,592	$ 3,000	$ 88,617	$ 4,000	$ 40,106
54	$ 0	$ 107,722	$ 3,000	$ 96,198	$ 4,000	$ 46,312
55	$ 0	$ 113,108	$ 3,000	$ 104,158	$ 4,000	$ 52,827
56	$ 0	$ 118,763	$ 0	$ 109,366	$ 4,000	$ 59,669
57	$ 0	$ 124,702	$ 0	$ 114,834	$ 4,000	$ 66,852
58	$ 0	$ 130,937	$ 0	$ 120,576	$ 4,000	$ 74,395
59	$ 0	$ 137,483	$ 0	$ 126,604	$ 4,000	$ 82,314
60	$ 0	$ 144,358	$ 0	$ 132,935	$ 4,000	$ 90,630
61	$ 0	$ 151,576	$ 0	$ 139,581	$ 4,000	$ 99,361
62	$ 0	$ 159,154	$ 0	$ 146,560	$ 4,000	$ 108,530
63	$ 0	$ 167,112	$ 0	$ 153,888	$ 4,000	$ 118,156
64	$ 0	$ 175,468	$ 0	$ 161,583	$ 4,000	$ 128,264
65	$ 0	$ 184,241	$ 0	$ 169,662	$ 4,000	$ 138,877
66	$ 0	$ 193,453	$ 0	$ 178,145	$ 0	$ 145,821
67	$ 0	$ 203,126	$ 0	$ 187,052	$ 0	$ 153,112
68	$ 0	$ 213,282	$ 0	$ 196,405	$ 0	$ 160,767
69	$ 0	$ 223,946	$ 0	$ 206,225	$ 0	$ 168,806
70	$ 0	$ 235,143	$ 0	$ 216,536	$ 0	$ 177,246
71	$ 0	$ 246,901	$ 0	$ 227,363	$ 0	$ 186,108
72	$ 0	$ 259,246	$ 0	$ 238,731	$ 0	$ 195,414
73	$ 0	$ 272,208	$ 0	$ 250,668	$ 0	$ 205,185
74	$ 0	$ 285,818	$ 0	$ 263,201	$ 0	$ 215,444
75	$ 40,000	$ 300,109	$ 60,000	$ 276,362	$ 80,000	$ 226,216

As you can see from The Magic of Starting Early chart, Ashley has almost a $30,000 investment balance by the time Lilly saves her first $3,000. Maddy saved double the amount Ashley saved, but because she waited until she was 45, her savings never reached the same level as Ashley or Lilly.

139

Both Lilly and Maddy saved significantly more money than Ashley, but the extra savings couldn't make up for the lost time—the money compounding effect it provides.

Time can't be saved. Once it is gone, it's gone. And saving more money later might not make up for it—like in this example. Maddy saved twice as much as Ashley, but ends up with almost $75,000 less.

While Maddy had more income at age 45, she also had no savings habit. Starting to save a significant portion of her income was like trying to lose 100 pounds. It required a huge shift in her lifestyle and habits. The new spending and saving habits don't come naturally to her because she's spent the last 20 years spending all of her income, plus some. It not only required more money, but also more effort and energy than if she had established good money habits early in life.

Ashley had less money but she took advantage of two key components—time and habit. As a result, she ended up with significantly more money in the end. Ashley used her youth and established sound money habits early in life. She can enjoy more in life as she gets older. Her habits and discipline allow her options well beyond what you would expect from her moderate income.

How many situations can you spend less money but end up with more? Ashley didn't win the lottery or take big business risks. She let her discipline and money work for her. She used youth (time) and the magic of compound interest to build her wealth slowly.

Compound interest is where the interest you earned is added to your balance. Then this new combined balance, if invested, earns interest.

If both the balance and interest are left in investments, the earnings compound month after month, year after year. It becomes a money generator.

The more years your money and interest are invested, the more it grows. It is like Ashley has a magic piggy bank. The money inside adds to itself and becomes more than what was put in it. No wonder Albert Einstein said compound interest is the eighth wonder of the world!

There was nothing flashy or dramatic about it. Ashley slowly saved money and let her money work for her. No wonder this strategy doesn't get much attention these days. It is boring and dull. Spending is celebrated more in our society than saving. No one snap chats a picture of their deposit slip or a bank statement showing a gain in their investment account.

When personal finance does get attention, it is usually in a negative light.

"I'm so broke."

"I have too much debt."

"The market is down."

"The economy is bad."

These poor me statements are just a few of the negative comments frequently shared. The same girls who make these comments are the ones who rave about their new handbags and gush over high-priced coats and over-the-top heels.

There are no big celebrations or social media posts for saving $167 each month. But there are plenty of posts of expensive meals and cocktails.

Like a healthy diet, it can be hard at first. It doesn't fit into our social norms. It is the simple life habits, like eating a balanced diet and getting exercise, that everyone knows but few actually do. Like a diet, good savings and spending habits get easier with each passing month. And eventually you get to the point where it takes very little thought or effort.

Saving early not only unleashes the magic of compounding interest, but it provides a buffer against market downturns. If you invest and are able to let your savings grow, you are better positioned to withstand the ups and downs of the market. If you are playing catch-up and only have a short time to accumulate, a downturn in the market will have a more significant impact. This is a big risk for Maddy's savings because she doesn't have the luxury of time to rebound from losses. If the market doesn't recover quickly, she has a smaller chance of being able to recover simply because she doesn't have the time needed to do so. An ill-timed bad downturn could mean the difference between having a comfortable nest egg and struggling financially for years.

Waiting to start your savings is not only risky; it limits your options. The math doesn't change but your age always will. Waiting to save for any reason is procrastination. It wastes one of the best and least expensive resources you have—**time**.

According to a 2013 survey by PNC Management, "saving early and regularly" was the most commonly (56%) reported factor of success by adults with $1 million in investments.[1] Controlling spending and smart investment choices tied at 38% in the same survey.[2] Only 26% indicated earning a lot of money as a success factor.

Think of it this way: if you save $160 each month from age 25 to 65, you will have a half million dollars ($500,000). Add a little more along the way and you will have over one million in the same time frame, if not sooner. These figures are based on a moderate 6 percent interest rate. Better rates will result in a bigger nest egg, which could mean a career break or an earlier retirement.

The biggest reason to start saving early is because time is on your side, but ONLY if you use it. The earlier you start to save, the less you'll have to save. The younger you are, the more you can take advantage of the time value of money and the magic of compound interest.

Whether it is for retirement or any other reason, saving while you are young pays off big when you are older!

Chapter 15
Understand Your Retirement Accounts

*It takes a great deal of courage to stand up to your
enemies, but even more to stand up to your friends.*

J.K. Rowling

Understanding your retirement account isn't about reading
the fine print. It is about understanding your options so you
can take advantage of the "Retirement Sale." The U.S. government encourages its citizens to save for their own retirement.
To motivate people to do it, they give them a big break on
taxes.

With more and more self-funded retirements, the idea of
working full-time until age 65 is outdated. For some, it is far
too long. For others, it isn't long enough. Even for those who
want to work their whole life, there often comes a day when
we aren't able to work and will need to live without a paycheck. The best way to save for such a day is a retirement account.

The Retirement Accounts Comparison chart shows important
aspects of the two most common retirement accounts.

Retirement Accounts Comparison			
	Employer Sponsored 401(k)		**Individual Retirement Account**
Contribution Limits	$18,000 ($24,000 if 50 years or older)		$5,000 ($6,500 if 50 years or older)
Matching Contributions	Many employers will contribute matching funds up to a set amount with a vesting schedule.		None. It is all your contributions
Administration	Majority handled by employer and its benefits firm		Handled by you and the financial firm where you open the account
	Traditional	Roth	Traditional	Roth
Tax Treatment of Contributions	Pre-tax, taken out of your paycheck prior to taxes being applied	After-tax, taken out of your paycheck after taxes are applied	Tax deductible, subtracted from your taxable income on your annual tax return	No deductions allowed, Contributions are made with after-tax dollars
Tax Treatment of Growth	Tax deferred until withdrawn	Tax free if held at least 5 years and age 59 ½ +	Tax deferred until withdrawn	Tax free if held at least 5 years and age 59 ½ +
Tax Treatment of Withdrawals	Taxed as ordinary income at time of withdrawal	Tax free if held at least 5 years and age 59 ½ +	Taxed as ordinary income at time of withdrawal	Tax free if held at least 5 years and age 59 ½ +

* Income limits and other rules apply. Consult your benefit provider, administrating firm or tax advisor.
** Contribution limits are higher for those age 50 and older.
*** Contributions may by limited or not allowed for high income earners.

Contribution limits apply to qualified retirement accounts. You can contribute three times the amount in a 401(k) compared to an IRA. These are annual contribution limits, which is one more reason why waiting to take advantage of a retirement account isn't advised. Even with higher limits for those age 50 or older, these higher limits aren't enough to make up for lost years.

Matching contributions offered by many employers are a huge boost to your savings. It is hard to find a downside to free money. That said, I am always surprised by how many don't take advantage of it. Since an employer isn't involved with an IRA, no matching contributions are allowed.

Administration of a 401(k) plan has the benefit of an employer association, which often makes participation simple and easy. IRAs are also easy to setup but require a little more effort on your part. Most banks and financial firms offer them and are happy to assist with everything you need to set it up.

Taxation of Traditional versus Roth Options

Roth options became available in the late 1990's. According to research conducted by Aon Hewitt, half of all companies are currently offering a Roth account within their 401(k) plans.[1]

This same research also shows the number of participants opting for the Roth feature is increasing.

The question regarding whether to do a Roth or a traditional retirement plan involves many variables including when you want to pay your taxes, what your tax rate is now versus what your tax rate will be when you withdraw the money, and how long it will be before you expect to withdraw the money.

With traditional plans, contributions are pre-tax, meaning you don't pay tax on the money you contribute. Taxes are due when you take the money out, usually after you retire. With a Roth account, you pay taxes before you put the money into the account. When you take the money out you don't have to pay taxes as long as you follow the 5-year and after age 59½ rules.

With both the traditional plan and the Roth plan you have to pay taxes—the difference is when you pay them and what your tax rate is at the time. It is hard to guess what the government will do with taxes in the future. I find generally accepted logic often doesn't apply to how our collective elected officials make decisions. Your guess on future tax rates is as good as mine.

Any investment growth within a traditional account is taxable when it is withdrawn. Investment growth within a Roth account is generally not taxable. This is one of the biggest advantages of a Roth account. As we saw in the last chapter, a significant portion of an account balance is often investment growth. In Ashley's case, $260,000 of her total $300,000 balance was growth (87%). In a Roth account, that growth is not taxed. This is significant savings at almost any tax rate.

IRS rules limit your ability to contribute to a Roth IRA if your income is considered too high. For those filing as single, contributions start to phase out at an income of $117,000 and are completely disallowed at $132,000. For those who are married and filing jointly, contribution restrictions start with a combined income of $184,000 and completely phase out at $194,000. These limits change year-to-year with inflation (check with your plan administrator for current limits). High-income earners are often limited within a 401(k) plan as well but it is based on plan specifics. Your employer or plan administrator should let you know if such limits apply to you.

Using Ashley as an example, she is putting just over $100 into her 401(k) retirement account each pay period. Her employer doesn't currently offer a Roth option. By default, she takes advantage of the traditional 401(k) account. The full $100 goes into her account. No taxes are applied (owed) on the 401(k) contribution money until it is taken out in retirement. Since she is in the 25% tax bracket, Ashley would save 25 percent or $25 dollars with this option. I am over simplifying how taxes work here so you can see the concept; don't get bogged down or distracted by a difference of a few dollars.

If Ashley's employer offered a Roth option, she would likely select it. Her current income and therefore tax rate is relatively low. She expects to be earning more and to move into the higher tax rate in the future. With a moderate rate of return, she expects the majority of her account to be investment gains when she retires. Ashley doesn't plan to take out the money until after age 59.5 (well beyond the current 5-year minimum and past the penalty age). She figures it would be better to pay taxes on contributions today in order to avoid paying income taxes on a larger sum in retirement, which would include both her contributions and her investment gains.

The value or benefit of the traditional or Roth options are heavily dependent on your current tax bracket, what (if any) investment return you expect, and what you expect your tax bracket to be when you withdraw the money. Because there are income limitations and no one knows for sure what the tax rates will be in years to come, it is impossible to know for sure which option is best. However, it is clear that it is best to take advantage of an employer-sponsored retirement account; both the traditional and the Roth option provide tax advantages you can't get in standard savings or investment accounts. And, both help you save so you can be self-reliant in retirement.

There are a number of choices, options and limits when establishing a retirement account. We only talk about the two most common retirement accounts here. The **most important MUST-DO steps are:**

1. Establish a retirement account

2. Contribute on a regular basis

3. Select low-fee investments

When time is on your side, take advantage of it. You can make time work in your favor.

Don't let the decision process keep you from acting. It is FAR better to make a mistake while setting up and funding a retirement account than it is to NOT set up a retirement account at all. Failing to set one up is the biggest mistake of all. Even if you don't select the perfect option, **you are better off with an imperfect retirement account than you are with no retirement account.**

Chapter 16
Investing Terms You Need to Know

*To educate yourself about personal finance is
to empower yourself with the resources and tools
needed to help you achieve your goals.*

Lin-Manuel Miranda

Wardrobe Wisdom

The wisdom of a good wardrobe can apply to a good investment portfolio. This section covers some key terms to understand when considering investing. I use wardrobe analogies not to make light of the subject, but to relate them to every day decisions we all make. Like everything in this book, what is important is understanding and applying the concepts—not memorizing terms.

Risk describes the potential danger associated with something. In financial terms, low risk is associated with investments that aren't likely to fluctuate significantly in value. They generally don't lose value but they are also slow to gain value. They are considered safe, like a classic pair of jeans and basic t-shirt. On the other hand, a strapless red dress with a slit up the side is much higher risk. The results of wearing this dress could go really well or really bad. It is high-risk and would only be appropriate in limited situations. Some can rock this look while others would never be comfortable in it. A high-risk investment is similar. The upside is great but if you aren't comfortable with the prospect of a big loss, high risk investments aren't for you. Like the red dress, no matter how well it works for your friend, if you aren't comfortable in it, it isn't for you.

Mutual Funds pool money from many investors with a common investment objective and invest those funds in assets (commonly stocks and/or bonds) based on that objective. Some objectives are to invest in high-growth, riskier investments. Some objectives are for low-risk asset protection or income. Others are socially motivated, like clean energy funds. A good mutual fund is professionally managed and invests in multiple stocks, bonds or other assets. Since they generally invest in multiple assets, it is a form of diversification. Investing in a mutual fund that has 30 U.S. stocks allows you to benefit from being invested in 30 stocks without the hassle and risk of directly purchasing, tracking, and monitoring 30 separate stocks.

Many mutual fund firms classify the risk levels of all of their funds so you know how much risk you are assuming with that particular fund. They should also have resources to assist you in determining your risk tolerance. Take advantage of these resources. They will help you learn about investing and about your own tolerance. Since so much of our financial well-being is a result of our own behavior, the better you understand yourself, the better you'll be at managing your finances.

Dollar cost averaging is a financial term that simply means your costs average out if you consistently invest at regular intervals over a long period of time. The idea is that it is better to invest $100 every month than to invest $1,200 once a year.

If you invest monthly, you can expect some months the market will be up and you'll buy on the high-end, while other months the market will be down and you'll buy at the low-end. In theory, you will be better off than if you would have invested the same amount all on one day of the year instead of 12 different days throughout the year. You wouldn't expect to buy a year's worth of wardrobe on one day. Why would you want to invest a year's worth of savings on one day?

Dollar cost averaging not only reduces your risk by spreading out your investment overtime, it supports the establishment of good financial habits. Regardless of how much you make, strong financial habits will help you in all financial situations – boom or bust. Good financial habits are like healthy eating habits; they will pay off throughout your life. You'll not only feel good tomorrow but you'll have a higher chance of feeling good 20 years from now.

I'm a big fan of this regular savings method as much for the habit it establishes as for the averaging and market smoothing benefits. It takes the stress out of it and simply allows you to regularly save money. Keeping it simple will increase your odds of sticking with it. Investing a portion of each paycheck is a simple way to dollar cost average your savings. Investing a portion of every paycheck by its nature is dollar cost averaging.

Diversification describes having multiple options in multiple categories. You diversify your wardrobe so you have something suitable to wear for most weather conditions or social situations. Having snow boots, dress shoes, tennis shoes and sandals would give you an option for most conditions. In financial terms, diversification gives you different financial options in different situations. If you have diverse investments, you have investments in multiple risk categories and multiple industries and asset classes.

The intent behind diversifying your investments is to spread your risk over multiple categories/industries/risk classes.

Having some of your investments in real estate and some in the stock market is an example of diversification. The factors influencing the real estate market in the area of your property are likely different than the influences that drive the stock and bond markets. Of course, some factors such as interest rates will influence the value of both, but there are many factors that will impact one and not the other.

Having all your investments in the stock of one company is not diversified. However, investing in an S&P 500 index account[1] is less risky because it is diversified over 500 different stocks. Because the S&P 500 is comprised of very large U.S. based companies, adding small companies, bonds and international companies, in the right situations, is even better. Each of these categories may perform differently during different economic times.

Asset Allocation is how you diversify. It is simply a term to reference how you allocate or divide what you have over different categories. Like a wardrobe, you need to have clothes that are functional and cover you year around, so you need some shoes, shirts, pants and tops. Having only one pair of shoes and pants isn't enough. We need multiple items in each category for different situations.

Asset allocation strategies suggest you spread your investments over multiple risk categories to spread your risk. Most of us have clothes for hot summer nights and cold winter days. Similar to having clothes for the ups and downs of the thermometer, it is best to have investments for the ups and downs of the market.

The models, labels, and colors vary across companies and resources but they should all describe the risk spectrum. Don't get lost in the details. Find a blend you are comfortable with and will allow you to sleep well at night.

Short-term	Fixed Income	Balanced	Risky	High Risk

If you put all your savings into short-term or fixed income options (like cash or taxable bonds) you may not "lose" any money, but what you have may not grow enough to keep up with inflation. At the same time, chasing high returns is risky and could result in the loss of some or all of your money. A blend across the spectrum based on your comfort level and time horizon is a better strategy. The closer you are to needing the money (i.e., retirement, major purchase, etc.), the lower risk you want in your investments.

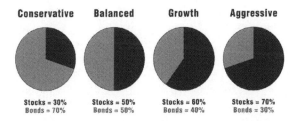

Conservative	Balanced	Growth	Aggressive
Stocks = 30% Bonds = 70%	Stocks = 50% Bonds = 50%	Stocks = 60% Bonds = 40%	Stocks = 70% Bonds = 30%

The asset blend pie charts are very general allocation models. A person with a long timeline and a high risk tolerance may want to have an aggressive growth blend of investments. This might include a mix of multiple bond mutual funds, along with a variety of growth focused stock funds. The growth model is a little less aggressive with more bond funds or other lower risk investments.

Those less comfortable with risk, or have a shorter investment time horizon (time until you plan to use the money), would be better suited for a balanced or conservative allocation model.

Index is like the one size fits all for a particular piece of clothing. It is an investment option that includes multiple kinds of investments within one. For example, the S&P 500 refers to the 500 different large U.S. stocks selected by Standard and Poor's (S&P).[2]Instead of representing one stock, the S&P 500 represents 500 stocks in multiple industries from fast food to oil production.

An index fund is a fund that invests in the underlying investments of the index it is associated with. So, a S&P 500 index fund would include all 500 of the stocks in the S&P 500. Instead of trying to predict or outperform the market, an index fund simply reflects the market segment it represents; in this case, the 5oo large U.S. stocks as determined by Standard and Poor's. Index funds generally have significantly lower fees.

Fees can quickly eat away at your money. In the words of John Oliver, in the June 13, 2016 Retirement Plans episode of Last

Week Tonight,[3] **"So think of fees like termites. They're tiny, they're barely noticeable and they can eat away your f#*& future."**

There is always a fee somewhere. Since your goal is to keep as much of your money as possible, you should know what the fees are and do everything you can to keep them under 1%.

If you aren't sure which funds to invest in, I suggest following the advice of one of the most successful investors in U.S. history, Warren Buffett. Warren Buffett is the 86-year-old CEO of Berkshire Hathaway. His net worth is estimated at $75 *billion*, making him the second riches person on earth. In the 2013 Berkshire Hathaway Annual Report, Buffett notes he has instructions in his will that the money left for his wife should be largely invested in a very low-cost S&P 500 index fund.[4] His preference is Vanguard's. If it is good enough for Warren Buffett and his family, it is good enough for me.

Recent announcements from Harvard University also support this strategy. According to the January 26, 2017 issue of Wall Street Journal,[5] over the past 10 years the S&P 500 total return outperformed Harvard University's actively managed endowment fund. If you had put money in the S&P 500 and left it there, you would have outperformed those who were presumably paid large sums of money to actively manage the Harvard University endowment.

Chapter 17
How Much Is Enough?

If you look at what you have in life, you'll always have more. If you look at what you don't have in life, you'll never have enough.

Oprah Winfrey

More Money = More Options

How much you need is in direct proportion to what you want to do and how long you want to do it. If you want to backpack across the country for a year and expect to only need $500 a month, $6,000 will do it (500 x 12 = 6,000). If you want to retire and need $50,000 a year to live, you'll need $1 million to $2 million assuming you'll live 20 to 40 years after you retire.

Let's say Ashley started to save even more once she pays off her student loan. Every year, she saves part of the raise she gets. She manages to accumulate over $500,000 by the time she is 65. A half a million dollars is a lot of money. Saving a large sum like this is a huge accomplishment!

But, the important question for Ashley is, is it enough for what she wants to do? If she wants to retire, maintain a house, and travel the world, it is likely not enough. If she wants to keep working and continue to save until she's 70, it likely is. Of course, lifestyle expectations, area cost of living, family circumstances, and health are all factors that play into the equation. Once again, the hard part isn't the math. The hard part is thinking through all the wants and what if's and putting a dollar amount to them.

This is the beauty of the basic budget and good spending habits. The same budget process Ashley used in her 20s will work in her 60s and all the years in between. The amounts will be different, but the basic categories still apply. The math equation is the same: income-expenses=gain or loss. As long as the loss per year is within range to sustain her savings, she's fine.

According to the National Center for Health Statistics, at age 65, a woman in the U.S. will live another 20 years on average.[1] That could be a long time if you have little income. If Ashley took $500,000 and put it into a low risk, low-interest account like CDs and withdrew a small portion each year, it would last a number of years. If Ashley can live on $25,000 a year plus what she might get in interest and from social security, she might be okay. But few can live on that amount today, let alone 40 years in the future. A typical rule of thumb is you will want 70% of your pre-retirement income in retirement.

A really safe strategy is to try to save enough money that when invested, it can generate an income for you. The Annual Income from Investment Interest chart shows a variety of investment amounts and interest rates. It is hard to get a 4% rate of return without risking the loss of your investment these days, but market conditions can change, so I want to show a variety of rates.

Annual Income from Investment Interest			
	Invested Amount		
Interest Rate	$250,000	$500,000	$1,000,000	$2,000,000
1%	$2,500	$5,000	$10,000	$20,000
2%	$5,000	$10,000	$20,000	$40,000
3%	$7,500	$15,000	$30,000	$60,000
4%	$10,000	$20,000	$40,000	$80,000

If you have $500,000 invested and it earns two percent interest each year, you can take the $10,000 interest earned each year and still have $500,000 left. With $2,000,000 invested at two percent, you could get $40,000 a year without drawing down your original investment.

Unlike the compound interest example where we saw Lilly, Ashley and Maddy reinvest their gains, this is an example of "simple" interest, where the interest/earnings may be spent each year and is not reinvested. Living only off of your interest is a lower-risk strategy, but it requires a large amount of savings to reach a comfortable income off of the simple interest.

There are a lot of financial calculators available online through your credit unions and banks. These are very helpful and have shown to help people better understand their savings needs. Ultimately, determining how much is enough is based on what you want to do and how long you want to do it. That is where your budget and smartphone calculator can once again get the job done.

Chapter 18
Don't Let Fear Sidetrack You

I will tell you the secret to getting rich
on Wall Street.
You try to be greedy when others are fearful.
And you try to be fearful when others are greedy.

Warren Buffett

Fear is a powerful emotion. And it is contagious. When fear strikes, our human instincts kick-in for fight or flight. Both fight and flight assumes quick action is required. This is when it is important to remember staying the course is as much of an action as making a change.

Everyone knows the rule: buy low and sell high. Sounds simple, and it is. That is, if you can keep fear and emotion out of it. However, most of us have a lot of emotions tied to our money so fear is a natural part of handling it. The truth is many people buy high and sell low, and fear is usually the underlying reason.

When the market is rising, we fear missing out and work up the courage to jump in and invest. This is usually about the time the market starts to correct and go down. As the market heads down, we panic and sell. The result is that we buy high and sell low, the classic recipe for losing money, not to mention stocking up on additional reasons to fear investing.

In the book *MONEY: Master the Game,* by Tony Robbins, Robbins highlights a study conducted by Fidelity.[1] Fidelity is a large and reputable mutual fund company. They looked at investors in their flagship mutual fund–Magellan. From 1977 to 1990 it had an average annual return of 29%. Twenty-nice percent is a fantastic return by almost any standard. Yet, Fidelity found the average person who invested in the fund actually lost money.

That's right.

On average those who invested in this great, high-performing mutual fund from a prominent financial firm actually lost money. Not because of the performance of the fund, but because of their own fear.

Fidelity found most Magellan investors lost money because they pulled their money out when the market went down (selling low) and put money back in when it went up (buying high).

They did the exact opposite of what the most fundamental rule of investing says to do. It wasn't for lack of understanding the rule or the fundamentals of the market. It was because emotions and timing got the best of them. The panic of one person impacts the emotional state of those around her. Add to it the contagious effect of fear and the constant buzz of "news" coverage reporting on every move in the market. Even when the market is up, half the headlines are about what to do when it goes back down again.

If you invest in the market, you have to keep the long-term in mind. Don't listen to the daily market reports. They are written for hype and ratings—not to make you rich. Regardless of their tagline or slogan, most investing shows are in business to entertain and sell ad spots, so they focus on stories that sell. The over-hyped market shows will not only drive you crazy, they will drive you to make poor financial decisions.

Fear is a fact of life. We all have it. The real secret isn't about avoiding or fighting your fear. It is about recognizing it and hitting pause when you sense it, evaluating before you react.

Research has shown money that was kept in the market resulted in a total balance **double** that of money that was out of the market for just 10 of the best days in the market. While this is a hypothetical situation, it demonstrates the dramatic impact of failing to have your money in the market for just a few of the best days (days with the highest gains). If you pull your money out and miss just ten of the biggest days of gains, you can cut your investments by more than half and take your average return down over two percent.

Attempts to time the market have repeatedly been proven to fail. They regularly perform worse than leaving money in the market. Yes, doing nothing regularly provides better results than actively moving money between investments.

I was first exposed to this effect when I was in the middle of my career. It struck me at the time what a dramatic impact panic could have. I am very grateful I learned this prior to the 2008 Great Recession. Like many, I was in the middle of my career, had two young kids and was saving for their college and my retirement at the same time. I was on the right track and feeling pretty good about it before the market took a nosedive.

As a mid-level staffer at a publicly traded financial institution, I probably paid more attention to the market than the average person. During the first few months of the downturn you could literally feel the shock and fear throughout the building. First, I watched the company stock plummet along with the rest of the market. My retirement account went with it. Then came salary cuts and regular rounds of layoffs. Some days I felt like throwing up in the garbage can under my desk.

Fortunately, I had seen a lot of historic data and intellectually knew trying to time the market regardless of its general direction was impossible. Making a rash decision out of panic was the worst thing I could do. But emotion can often overrule intellect.

I vividly remember having to stop myself from changing my 401(k) account out of fear. On paper (more accurately on a computer screen) it looked like I had "lost" half my retirement savings. But when I calculated how much I had actually put into my 401(k) over the years, the balance was still slightly above what I had put into it. Of course, the gains I had seen over the previous 10 years were gone, but I hadn't "lost" any of what I originally invested. This realization helped me keep calm. It also helped that I was years away from being able to retire, so I still had time on my side.

These two factors allowed me to hold tight and keep from changing my investment options. As a result, I enjoyed the strong gains from the recovery over the following nine years as the market rebounded.

I also continued to contribute to my retirement account during those historic lows. That allowed me to buy almost double the number of fund shares for the same dollar contribution I was making before the market crash.

It was a gut-wrenching time for everyone. Hopefully, we don't have another financial crisis for another 80 years. But one thing is for sure: The market will go up and down. The economy will go through more recessions and recoveries. Take time now to think about how you will handle it when the market goes down. If you do, you will be mentally prepared to handle it. A little planning for the worst can help you be at your best when needed.

The Other Side of Fear

Another fear related to our money is the fear of never having enough. You don't want fear to cause you to do something rash, but fear can also keep you from using and enjoying your money. What's the point of having it if you can't enjoy it?

This book is intended to help you minimize financial mistakes, avoid some common pitfalls and position yourself for financial security. The result should be a sense of power, control and comfort. But taken too far, watching your money could turn you into a control freak. That's not good for anyone—you or those around you. Watch your money, but avoid taking it to the extreme where you turn into a miser like Ebenezer Scrooge in the Charles Dickens's classic, A Christmas Carol.[2]

In this classic tale, Ebenezer spends all his time and energy controlling and counting his money. He misses out on personal relationships and connecting with people around him because he fears someone will take his money or he won't have enough. Like all things in life, moderation is key. If you take financial control too far you will miss out on some of the great freedoms it provides.

There is a fine line between controlling your money and being controlled by your money. It is a personal line we all must learn to draw for ourselves.

Chapter 19
What's It To You?

*Wealth after all is a relative thing since
he that has little and wants less is richer than he
that has much and wants more.*

Charles Caleb Colton

What's It Look Like to You?

What does financial security mean to you? What about financial freedom? Is it avoiding debt or getting out of debt? Is it having enough to pay your bills every month and cash flowing Christmas? Is it having enough to make a career leap? Or maybe it is the simple security of knowing you can take care of yourself if needed?

Financial security means something different to everyone. Some are happy with a tiny house and few obligations. Others want big checking accounts so they can donate to make the world better one cause at a time. It isn't about the math or a specific amount sitting in an account. It is about freedom and the flexibility it provides.

What it looks like and how much it will take for you is what is important. It might be enough to cover rent, a better car and yoga in the park. Or it might be having enough in the bank that you can take a year off to volunteer for your favorite charity.

For my Mom, it was being financially independent. It must have looked impossible to her at first. She was 37 years old when she kicked out my father for the sake of her kids and her own sanity. She had no money and multiple debts from the marriage.

Her first goal was to earn enough to pay the bills and keep a roof over our heads. Her second goal was to get out of debt. Her third was to save up for a home of her own. Those are very ambitious goals for a middle-aged, single mother of three making just over minimum wage.

But with grit, determination, and hard work, she accomplished all three of her goals. It took 18 years of steady hard work. With each small step, she gained confidence in herself and her abilities.

At age 54 she bought her own home. She delighted in picking out every detail and weighing the cost of each feature of HER home. Despite extensive medical problems, she managed to stay out of debt, except for her home and car. When she passed away at age 62, she had built-up enough equity in her home to leave her three grown children a small inheritance.

She didn't meet these goals because of a formula or set plan. She achieved them because of what they meant to her and the daily choices, big and small, she made that eventually provided the lifestyle she dreamed of having, one that allowed her to make her own choices.

As her daughter, the material things she left me are treasures. But the lessons she taught me and the example she set was by far the most valuable thing a parent could give a child.

I watched her make countless decisions along the way. Some days were *really* tough. Juggling a job, three children, a home and the endless bills that came with all of it. It wasn't glamorous or fun, but little by little she gained ground. Little by little she gained her independence. Little by little she gained respect for herself and the respect of those around her. In hindsight, I now see that for Mom financial security was about how it made her feel—not about the material things it provided.

It was those tough days as a young girl watching her struggle and fight that had the biggest impact on me. They are some of the strongest memories I have from my youth. For me, financial security is having the luxury of making life decisions based on what's right for me and my family, instead of on need, like my mom.

What Does It Mean to You?

Take a minute to think about what financial security looks like to you. How would it feel? What would be different?

If you are already financially secure, what does financial abundance look like to you? What dreams would you accomplish or gifts would you give if you had the money?

What steps can you take today to help you get there? What spending habits could you adjust to help make your dreams come true? How much can you save if you really put your mind to it?

Take the next three minutes to jot down your financial dreams. No judging yourself or your dreams in the process. Just jot down what financial freedom looks like for you. Have fun with it.

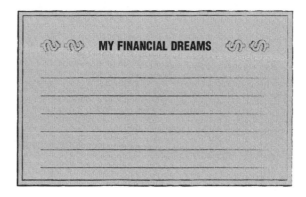

MY FINANCIAL DREAMS

A dream becomes a goal the minute you start taking action to move toward it. Your grit and determination is in proportion to your goals and how badly you want to accomplish them. The more important your goal is to you, the more likely you are to achieve it.

Take a minute to jot down what will be different in your life when you accomplish these goals. What will you no longer have to do? What will you start doing that you don't do now?

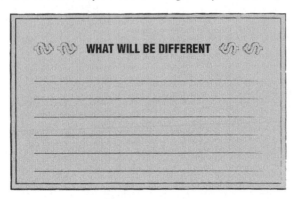

WHAT WILL BE DIFFERENT

What habits will you establish to help you achieve your goals? What are the triggers that will prompt your financial routines? What will your routines be? Equally as important as the routine itself, what will be your reward? It is the reward that supports the habit. In his book *The Power of Habit*, Charles Duhigg explores in detail the science behind habits and the important role they play in our everyday lives.[1] He explains that each habit has a trigger, routine and reward. What will your habits look like? Here are a couple that come to mind for me.

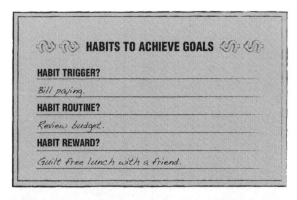

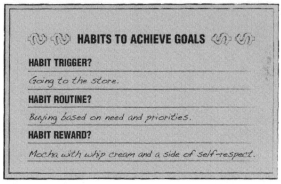

What can you do this week and this month to get you closer to your goals? Are there automatic transfers or direct deposit changes you can make that will help? Are there adjustments to your spending or your budget you want to make? What can you do now to help you reach your goals in the coming months and years?

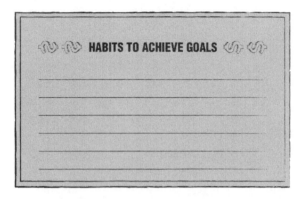

Just like a change jar on your dresser that collects spare change but over time adds up to a $100, small financial action steps add up over time.

Your budget, credit score and calculator are tools to help along the way, but **it is your passion and persistence that will get you there.**

As your debt goes down and your savings accounts grow, so will your financial confidence. You will question promotional claims about products and pricing, and you won't spend your money unless there is clear value for you. You will be a savvy shopper not easily swayed by "sales," ads, or a spokesperson. You will discover the joy of having enough for what is important to you. You will experience the freedom of making choices solely based on what is right for you. And in turn, you will set an example for others.

The concepts, tools and information in this book are here to help guide you, but **the journey is yours.** Where you go and how you get there will be determined by how you apply these tools and concepts in your life.

What You Need for the Journey

No matter how big your goal, applying these rules can get you there.

- Goals and the determination to pursue them

- A basic calculator
- Financial concepts and tools provided in this book

Net Worth ≠ Personal Worth

Remember, your value to the world has nothing to do with your account balance or your personal income.

It is worth repeating. NEVER confuse your personal worth with your net worth. Your personal worth is made up of who you are; a person of character, a loyal friend, a hard worker, an avid supporter of what is right. The second is a dollar figure, a figure that will fluctuate. It may provide you freedom. It cannot provide you happiness.

Control Your Bottom Line

By mastering this key equation, you control your financial score board:

Income – Expenses = Gain or Loss

Establish Sound Habits

Sound hygiene habits improve your health. Sound money habits improve your finances.

Pay yourself first. Even if it is only a few dollars, establishing and sticking with a savings habit has an amazing long-term impact.

Shop Smart. Ask questions and educate yourself. You are your own best advocate.

Protect your credit like you would protect your personal reputation.

Make your money work for you. It is better to earn interest than to pay interest. Harness the magic of compound interest to transform your regular savings into a substantial nest egg.

This book is intended for you to get started on a path of financial health and wellness. It isn't the finishing line, but the starting point. Armed with these concepts and tools, you can establish the habits to achieve a lifetime of goals. I look forward to seeing a future filled with wise women making financial decisions right for them and their personal goals.

Enjoy the journey!

Section 4
Tidbits and Resources

A woman with a voice is by definition a strong woman. But the search to find that voice can be remarkably difficult.

Melinda Gates

Chapter 20
Time is Money, Spend it Wisely

Time is money.

Benjamin Franklin

For most people, their time is their biggest asset. This is especially true for the young. You trade your time for an employer's money and some benefits. It is important to make the most of what you are getting in trade for your time. Your skills and time are income-generating assets. They should be treated and protected as if they were precious jewels!

Sometimes the best job isn't the job or career with the biggest paycheck or best title, but the one with the best opportunity to live the lifestyle you want or provide the bridge to get you where you want to go.

One of my early college jobs was working in the gift shops at the Minneapolis/St. Paul airport. As I took more college classes, I needed to make the most of my time. So, I asked for more shifts in the duty-free shop. In the time between flights, business was slow, which meant I could sit in the packaging area and read. The money wasn't great, but the fact that I could study made it worth it. When they later instituted a no-reading rule, the value I was getting for my time went down.

I studied up on cocktailing and became a waitress. It was a hard job to get at the airport, but I convinced management I could do it. This was a great college job. The shifts were flexible. If you worked hard and did a good job, you were usually well compensated for it. The switch to waitressing allowed me to make more money in fewer hours, which allowed me more time to study and a bit more cash to offset living expenses.

Part of the cost/benefit calculation for any job should also include the side costs and benefits of the job. Side costs would include things like commute (both time and money spent to do so), parking expenses, dress requirements, or expectations. Side benefits include training and education provided, travel, or a provided company car.

If a job requires a long commute and parking expenses, but the pay and other benefits are the same as a closer position without the added commuting expense, you are better off with the closer job. This is not only due to the added cost for commuting expenses, but also because it takes more of your time. If it is a per-hour job, you could spend more time working and earning than commuting. Thus, a double win: Less cost and more time or earning potential. Other benefits to consider is what experience you are gaining or what skills you are learning. One of the side benefits to my waitressing position at the Minneapolis/St. Paul airport was that I had the opportunity to meet and visit with business and professional people that I would otherwise not have been able to meet. This allowed me to see and observe how experienced business people handled themselves. Through my job, I learned how to behave as a business professional. This had value not only because of the education, but also the inspiration. I met wonderful people who inspired me to keep working on my degree, to apply for the prestigious internships, and set goals. This side benefit of the job was invaluable. Since my interests and college program were focused on the business world, this was of huge value to me. It was over 25 years ago, but to this day I still remember some of the interesting people I met and conversations I had while serving cocktails and making money to pay rent.

Another valuable lesson I learned in that position was if I focused on providing good service, I would leave with more tips than if I focused on making money. It seems like a minor detail, but time after time it proved true. If I focused on doing my job right, I would be rewarded. If I focused on making money, I was always disappointed.

This has carried forward into all the jobs that followed. If I went into a meeting with a focus on what I wanted to get out of it, there was often little progress. But, if I walked into the same meeting with a focus on reaching a clear business objective outside of my wants and needs, I would walk out with solutions.

Now that I have kids of my own, I suggested they look at their time the same way. When my daughter was in the second semester of her freshman year in college, my husband and I told her she needed to get a job or do something where she could gain experience. She worked during college breaks to help offset living expenses, so we were hoping she would focus more on gaining experience than earning money, ideally in an area related to the field she was studying. This way, she would be learning about her chosen field, which is often more important than the wage generally offered around most college campuses.

When employers review a resume, they look at two things: knowledge (often demonstrated through education, degrees or certificates) and skill/actual experience. Experience tells an employer you not only have the needed knowledge but you can apply it. Knowing a programing language is one thing, but building a working web site and associated functions that make the web site work is a whole different level. Ultimately, it is the application of knowledge that is valuable to a company and a boss. It is where the rubber meets the road and your true worth to an enterprise is shown.

Another big side benefit of a position is where it can get you. When I started working for a small niche market insurance company, I had the opportunity to learn about every aspect of an organization. I was paid to learn the details of the industry and was rewarded when I applied this knowledge to help the company grow.

When my husband took a position in another town I had knowledge, experience, and a recommendation letter I could take to other prospective employers in this new community. It opened doors for me and landed me a job with a large and growing financial institution. This position not only gave me more skills and career opportunities, but it is where I learned a lot about finance and the importance of saving and investing. I got paid to learn about finance. I had the opportunity to travel, to work with amazing people, and move into jobs I never knew existed prior to joining the company.

When you are looking for positions, look for where you can best apply your talents and what you can gain from it–not only in compensation, but in experience, new skills, new networks and exposure. Look beyond the pay and benefits and look for the opportunities it may offer.

Chapter 21
Wisdom of the Ages

He who loses money, loses much;
He who loses a friend, loses much more;
He who loses faith, loses all.

Eleanor Roosevelt

Take Their Advice

If reading my advice in this book didn't quite get through to you, please take the advice of these savvy, successful women, all of whom I admire and respect. Names may have been changed to protect the smart and savvy.

Jenn is a mom and successful business owner. Her advice is, "Save a little every pay check. It adds up. Ideally, you do it with direct deposit so you aren't tempted to spend it once it's in your pocket."

Abby is a wife, mom and apartment complex owner and manager. Her advice is, "Spend more time researching and picking a roommate than picking an apartment. If your roommate flakes, you are still on the hook for your lease and other commitments."

Aunt Betty is a retired businesswoman who grew up in an era when women had very few career options. Her advice, "Save, Save, Save."

Nancy is a working mom who made an impressive career in a traditionally male-dominated industry while being genuine and graceful. Her advice is, "Learn and apply yourself. If you do, you will always be able to find someone to pay you."

Stephanie is a mom, wife and executive. Her advice is, "Don't be afraid to say, 'That's not a priority for me right now.' We've all been in those conversations with a friend or family member, and you get talking about buying or wanting this or that. The next thing you know, you've talked yourself into spending double what you wanted to spend. It is one thing if you are talking about a fruity drink or purse, but it is often the summer vacation or major purchase. The more honest you are with yourself and friends, the easier managing your money is. Don't let a casual conversation derail your long-term plans."

Mary is a wife, mother, coach and sassy friend. Her advice is, "Even if you live off a trust fund, you need to know how to manage money. Whether you inherit $100 or $100,000, you need to know how to manage it wisely or it will soon be gone."

Molly is a wife and successful medical technology professional. Her advice is, "Don't count on inheritance. The last few years of life are expensive and ate up a lot of my parent's resources. It is great if you get it, but hoping for inheritance is a bad financial plan!"

She goes on to share, "A year after my mother died, I received a small check from the sale of her home. It came with a lot of emotions. To me, it was my mom's legacy. To my husband, it was just money.

It was important to me we did something with it that was long lasting, something Mom would have had pride in if she were alive. We put it toward real estate to help position us to be financially independent.

In my state, inheritance is not a marital asset unless it is put into a joint account. Had I not felt secure in my marriage I would not have put it into a joint account or used it to pay down debt on a mortgage with both our names on it. I also felt that not applying it to the financial goals my husband and I shared would have been a betrayal of our relationship."

Chapter 22
Tools and Resources

Money is only a tool.
It will take you wherever you wish,
but it will not replace you as the driver.

Ayn Rand

Tools to Help Along the Way

Technology trends may change the details of how we move, store, track and exchange money. Even what we call it may change as technology evolves, but humans have been exchanging things of value for products and services since we have occupied the earth. I am confident the principles and concepts in this book will apply, regardless of the technology. From the abacus to the app, the math is the same–add, subtract, multiply and divide. The core financial concepts here will help you navigate the financial aspect of life through every age, regardless of the labels and the technology used to manage it.

- For any bills not setup for automatic payment, set a calendar reminder for paying them. It helps keep you organized and protects against forgetting if something comes up, which in turn helps protect your credit score.

- Calculators

  o Smartphone or dime store calculators can do most of the math you need.

  o Financial calculators available through credit unions, banks, or other financial web sites can do the calculations your smartphone calculator can't. They can also do some interesting "how" calculations. Things like: how much will my savings be worth? How many years will it take to pay off a loan? How long will it take to pay off my credit card?

  o Student Loan Calculators are available with most of the financial calculators noted above, but I like some of the following calculators that specifically address college debt.

  o Loan Payment Calculator www.iowastudentloan.org/private-student-loans/loan-payment-calculator.aspx. While the information may be state specific, the math used by the calculator is going to be the same regardless of where you live or attend school.

  o Debt to Salary Calculator at Mapping Your Future. www.mappingyourfuture.org/paying/debtwizard

  o Starting Salaries by college majors can be found at www.payscale.com/college-salary-report-2013/majors-that-pay-you-back

  o Financial Apps are rapidly growing in number. I use a few available through the financial firms where I have accounts. I have also heard good things about a few third-party personal financial apps and have looked into a few. I haven't yet found one that provides enough added value for me to justify the personal information I would have to share.

Recommended Reads and Resources

Personal finance is a large subject with many aspects. This book is intended to get you started, provide you with the basics, and help you avoid some common mistakes. I encourage you to learn more. With that in mind, here are some books, radio shows, articles and podcasts to get you started. To show I walk the talk, I included a few that focus more on personal worth than net worth.

- I think *The Confidence Code: The Science and Art of Self-Assurance—What Women Should Know* is a must-read for every young woman. Authors Katty Kay and Claire Shipman do an outstanding job examining and explaining the importance of having confidence. Kay, Katty and Shipman, Claire. "The Confidence Code." New York: Harper-Collins, 2014

- Brzenzinski, Mika, *"Knowing Your Value: Women, Money, and Getting What You're Worth"* New York: Weinstein Books, 2010.

- Stanley, Thomas J. *Millionaire Women Next Door; The Many Journeys of Successful American Business Women.* Kansas City: Andrews McMeel Publishing, August 1, 2005.

- Brown, Brené, Ph.D., L.M.S.W. *"The Gifts of Imperfection: Let Go of Who You Think You're Supposed to Be and Embrace Who You Are"* Minneapolis: Hazelden Information & Educational Services, 2010.

- John Oliver in the June 12, 2016 Retirement Plans episode of Last Week Tonight on HBO. "Episode 74." Last Week Tonight with John Oliver, HBO.

- Malcolm Gladwell's podcast Revisionist History is a great program. I'm a fan of his work, but in particular I suggest listening to the episode on thresholds and how our human nature will pick being liked over being right if the social pressure is strong enough. Gladwell, Malcom. Revisionist History (Audio Podcast). Retrieved from www.itunes.apple.com

- *Money: Master the Game,* by Tony Robbins is a deep dive into investing for the long term. Robins, Tony. Money Master the Game Seven Simple Steps to Financial Freedom. New York: Simon & Schuster, 2014.

- Dave Ramsey radio show and corresponding free podcasts. I enjoy hearing all the different situations callers from across the country get into and how they are working to resolve them. It is entertaining. The Dave Ramsey Show.

- Money Talk with Bob Brinker. I like to listen to the radio while doing work around the house. If it is Sunday afternoon, this is my pick. You can find a list of stations the show airs on at www.bobbrinker.com. Very sage advice. His focus is investing for the long term.

- My web site, AGirlsGuidetoPersonalFinance.com has resources and information that I couldn't fit into this book.

Your Actual Budget (where you are now)

Monthly Income & Deductions

	Gross Income (before taxes and deductions)
	- Pre-tax Retirement Savings (i.e., traditional 401(k))
	- Health Insurance and other pre-tax deductions
	Subtotal (pre-tax)
	- After-tax Retirement Savings (i.e., Roth 401(k))
	- Taxes
	- After-tax deductions
	Net Monthly Income (net pay x paychecks per month)

Monthly Expenses

Housing

	Rent/Mortgage
	Utilities (water, electric, heating, trash, etc.)
	Phone
	Cable, internet, etc.
	Insurance

Transportation

	Car/Transportation (car, bus, train, Uber)
	Car Insurance (annual premium divided by 12)
	Gas & Maintenance

Debt/Loans

	Student Loans (total monthly payment of all loans)
	Credit Card Debt (Any balance over 30 days old)
	Personal Loans or Retail Debt

General Living

	Groceries & Home Essentials
	Medical (Rx, co-pays, wellness items)
	Clothing
	General Living/Miscellaneous

Non-essentials

	Entertainment (eating out, girls' night, movies)
	Charity
	Miscellaneous (gifts, Girl Scout cookies, just because)

Savings

	Life Happens Fund
	Emergency Fund then to Debt Reduction
	Mid and Long-term Goals (grad school, vehicle, etc.)
	Total Monthly Expenses

	Gain or Loss

Your Desired Monthly Budget

Monthly Income & Deductions

	Gross Income (before taxes and deductions)
	- Pre-tax Retirement Savings (i.e., traditional 401(k))
	- Health Insurance and other pre-tax deductions
	Subtotal (pre-tax)
	- After-tax Retirement Savings (i.e., Roth 401(k))
	- Taxes
	- After-tax deductions
	Net Monthly Income (net pay x paychecks per month)

Monthly Expenses

Housing (20 - 35%)

	Rent/Mortgage
	Utilities (water, electric, heating, trash, etc.)
	Phone
	Cable, internet, etc.
	Insurance

Transportation (10-15%)

	Car/Transportation (car, bus, train, Uber)
	Car Insurance (annual premium divided by 12)
	Gas & Maintenance

Debt/Loans (0-20%)

	Student Loans (total monthly payment of all loans)
	Credit Card Debt (Any balance over 30 days old)
	Personal Loans or Retail Debt

General Living (20-40%)

	Groceries & Home Essentials
	Medical (Rx, co-pays, wellness items)
	Clothing
	General Living/Miscellaneous

Non-essentials (5-20%)

	Entertainment (eating out, girls' night, movies)
	Charity
	Miscellaneous (gifts, Girl Scout cookies, just because)

Savings (10-50%)

	Life Happens Fund **Bare Minimum $25**
	Emergency Fund then to Debt Reduction
	Mid and Long-term Goals (grad school, vehicle, etc.)
	Total Monthly Expenses

	Gain or Loss

Notes

CHAPTER 1: Why Money Matters

1. Bureau of Labor Statistics, U.S. Department of Labor, *Economics Daily*, Women's Earnings Compared to Men's Earnings in 2014. www.bls.gov/opub/ted/215/womens-earnings-compared-to-mens-earnings-in-2014. Accessed January 19, 2017.

2. Johnston Taylor, Susan. "The Pink Tax: Why Women's Products Often Cost More." www.money.us.com/money/personalfinancearticles/2016-02-17.

3. Ernest & Young, "The Groundbreaker Series: Driving Business Through Diversity", 2009, page 6, Boston Consulting Group Report 2009.

CHAPTER 2: What Money Is and What It Isn't

1. Stanley, Thomas J. Millionaire Women Next Door; The Many Journeys of Successful American Business Women. Kansas City: Andrews McMeel Publishing, August 1, 2005.

SECTION 2: Keeping What You Earn

1. Stanley, Thomas J. Stop Acting Rich; And Start Living Like a Real Millionaire. Hoboken: John Wiley & Sons, Inc., 2009.

CHAPTER 6: Credit – Know the Score

1. Financial Calculator. "How Long Will it Take to Pay Off my Credit Card?" www.timevalue.com.

2. "Swipe Fees" www.nrf.com/advocacy/policy-agenda/swipe-fees.

3. FICO. www.fico.com.
   Equifax. www.equifax.com.
   Experian. www.experian.com.
   Transunion. www.transunion.com.

4. FICO. www.fico.com.

5. Id.

6. Annual Credit Report Request Service, P.O. Box 105281, Atlanta, Georgia, 30348, www.annualcreditreport.com.

CHAPTER 7: Where to Keep Your Money

1. Paycheck, Johny: Nashville Edition. "Take this Job and Shove It." New York City: Epic, 1977.

CHAPTER 9: Shop Smart

1. Wilson, Gretchen: Rucker, Allen. "Redneck Woman: Stories from my Life." New York: Grand Central Publishing, 2007.

CHAPTER 10: Assets versus Liabilities

1. "Fast Facts." www.nces.ed.gov/fastfacts/display. Accessed 1/22/2017

2. Crutsinger, Martin. "Most American Households Doing Better Financially." www.dailyherald.com/article/20160525. Accessed 1/22/2017.

3. www.usnews.com/education.

4. Picchy, Amy. "Congrats, Class of 2016: You're the Most Indebted Yet." Money Watch. May 4, 2016.

CHAPTER 11: Big Buys

1. www.edmunds.com
2. www.kbb.com
3. www.edmunds.com
4. www.consumerreports.org Subscription required.
5. www.zillow.com/mortgage-learning-closing-costs

CHAPTER 13: Insure for a Good Night's Sleep

1. www.healthcare.gov
2. www.wikipedia.org/wiki/vehicle_insurance_in_the_Unit ed_States. Accessed 1/22/17.

CHAPTER 14: The Magic of Saving and Investing

1. PNC Wealth Management. "Wealth and Value Survey being Wealthy." January 2014.
2. Id.

CHAPTER 15: Understand Your Retirement Accounts

1. "AON Hewitt Analysis Finds More Employers Adding Roth Features to Expand Savings Options." www.aon.mediaroom.com. April 28, 2014

CHAPTER 16: Investing Terms You Need to Know

1. S & P Jones Indices. S & P 500. www.us.spindices.com/indices/equity/sp-500. Standard & Poor's 500 is a stock market index using the market capitalization of 500 of the largest companies having common stock listed on the NYSE or NASDAQ.
2. Id.
3. "Episode 74," Last Week Tonight with John Oliver, HBO.
4. Berkshire Hathaway Inc. "2013 Annual Report." P.20.
5. Chung, Juliet, and Dawn Lim. "Harvard Outsources Endowment." The Wall Street Journal. January 26, 2017, p.B1

CHAPTER 17: How Much Is Enough?

1. Arias, Elizabeth, Changes in Life Expectance by Race and Hispanic Origin in the United States, 2013-2014, National Center for Health Statistics Data Brief No. 244, April 2010

CHAPTER 18: Don't Let Fear Sidetrack You

1. Robins, Tony. Money Master the Game Seven Simple Steps to Financial Freedom. P.400. New York: Simon & Schuster, 2014.

2. Dickens, Charles. "A Christmas Carol." New York: Watermill, 1994.

CHAPTER 19: What's It To You?

1. Duhigg, Charles. The Power of Habit Why We Do What We Do in Life and Business. New York: Random House, 2012

Acknowledgements

This book would not be possible without the help and support of many people.

To my amazing husband, Doug, I could not have done this without you.

To my daughter and son, you two are my pride and joy.

To my sister, Lori, thank you for letting me tell my story.

To my friends who encouraged me along the way, I cannot tell you how much it has meant to me.

To Chad Tramp and Scott Fiene, thank you for helping me make the important but sometimes difficult points.

Finally, to the other authors who shared their wisdom, thank you for sharing your lessons learned.

About the Author

Nanette Joell (Joey) Beech was raised by a divorced mother who wanted a better life for her daughter. She instilled in Joey the importance of managing her money, and the importance of being financially independent, so she could make her own choices.

Joey has over 25 years of professional experience, much of which was in the financial industry. She received a Bachelor's of Science degree from the University of Minnesota – Twin Cities.

Joey was raised in the Midwest and continues to live there with her husband of over 25 years. They have two grown children.

Learn more at:

AGirlsGuidetoPersonalFinance.com

@GirlsGuide2Finance

Facebook.com/JoeyBeechAuthor

Made in the USA
Monee, IL
28 December 2019